Effective Problem-Solving

Developing Management Skills

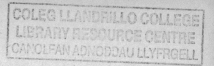

Developing Management Skills

EFFECTIVE PROBLEM-SOLVING

David A Whetten
Kim Cameron
Mike Woods

HarperCollins*Publishers*

This edition first published in 1996 by
HarperCollins College
An imprint of HarperCollins Publishers Ltd, UK
77-85 Fulham Palace Road
Hammersmith
London W6 8JB

Mike Woods asserts the moral right to be identified as the author of the
adapted material.

British Library Cataloguing in Publication Data. A catalogue record for this
book is available from the British Library

ISBN 0-00-4990439

Typeset by Dorchester Typesetting Group Ltd
Printed and bound by Scotprint Ltd, Musselburgh
Cover design: The Senate

Other Titles in the Series

Effective Conflict Management
Effective Stress Management
Effective Motivation
Effective Empowerment and Delegation
Effective Communication

Other Titles in the Series

Effective Conflict Management
Effective Stress Management
Effective Motivation
Effective Empowerment and Delegation
Effective Organization

Contents

Preface   ix

Introduction   1

Skill Pre-assessment   3
  Diagnostic Surveys for Creative Problem-Solving

Skill Learning   9
  Problem-Solving, Creativity and Innovation
  Steps in Rational Problem-Solving
  Limitations of the Rational Problem-Solving Model
  Impediments to Creative Problem-Solving
  Conceptual Blocks
  Conceptual Blockbusting
  Fostering Innovation
  Summary
  Behavioural Guidelines

Skill Analysis   81
  Case Involving Creative Problem-Solving

Skill Practice   85
  Exercise for Applying Conceptual Blockbusting

Skill Application   89
  Application Activities for Solving Problems Creatively

Scoring Key   91

Glossary   99

References   103

Index   107

Contents

Preface — ix

Introduction — 1

Step One: Self-assessment — 3
Diagnostic Surveys for Creative Problem-Solving

Skill Learning —
Problem Solving, Creativity, and Innovation
Steps in Rational Problem-Solving
Limitations of the Rational Problem-Solving Model
Impediments to Creative Problem-Solving
Conceptual Blocks
Conceptual Blockbusting
Fostering Innovation
Summary
Behavioural Guidelines

Skill Analysis —
Case Involving Creative Problem-Solving

Skill Practice —
Exercises for Applying Conceptual Blockbusting

Skill Application —
Application Activities for Solving Problems Creatively

Scoring Key — 91

Glossary — 99

References — 101

Index — 107

Preface

Effective Problem-Solving is one of a series of six books based on *Developing Management Skills for Europe*, a major work by David Whetton, Kim Cameron and Mike Woods. The other titles from the series are *Effective Conflict Management*, *Effective Communication*, *Effective Empowerment and Delegation*, *Effective Stress Management* and *Effective Motivation*. Presented in a convenient form they provide a background of reading and exercises for tutors and students taking MBA grade or other business qualifications.

Each book in the series seeks to find a balance between a sound theoretical background and case studies. Our objective remains, as it did in the combined work, to develop behavioural skills not only to increase knowledge and understanding in the area, but also to enable students to apply what they have learned. We hope our readers will achieve their qualifications and become productive members of their organisations by learning applicable skills.

The structure of the books and the method of teaching they employ are, in our opinion, unique. Each book begins with a series of questionnaires designed to check on the reader's present understanding of the area and in some cases, assist the reader in self assessment. Thus, in this book, *Effective Problem-Solving*, the reader is asked first to rate his or her aptitude in creative activities.

From these questionnaires the reader will be able to set learning objectives for the book and on finishing the text, see how much he or she has been able to relate to the very personal world of self.

The main body of the text provides a theoretical background to the issues of improving creative and rational problem-solving skills. The text closes with a case study, exercises and a section on Application Planning.

Our firm belief is that when 'all is said and done, there is more said than done'. We are asking our readers to make a real commitment to use the material and become more effective in their chosen professions.

Introduction

The words 'problem-solving' are in themselves jargon, but they have become so much part of the language of managers that it is easy to forget that they imply a special meaning only understood by a select band. Problem-solving, in the managerial context implies a logical process which is called upon when something out of the routine occurs or when something out of the routine is needed.

Imagine that you need to travel to a town X some 300 kilometres from your home. You intend to go by train and arrive at the station only to find that all trains have been cancelled due to an accident on the line. This, in anyone's language could be a problem. 'Problem-solving', as we will discuss it in this book, could be about what you do now. Suppose that for various reasons you need to reach your chosen destination, but that obvious alternatives are not possible – you cannot go by air, a car is not available.

You might begin thinking about the problem itself – WHY do I need to get X by such a time?

Then you might see WHAT could be done about each aspect of the problem – not doing anything, just thinking about it. For example:

■ You need to speak to Fred urgently – could you phone, fax or even write?

■ You need to understand how Fred feels – could you ring a friend, who is already in the picture, to see Fred and explain.

■ It would be nice to visit the exhibition of paintings in X before you come home – nice, but could you postpone the trip or perhaps miss out altogether?

■ Could you go later when the trains are running or your car will be available?

Prioritising or, much more likely, combining several of these solutions, you may devise a plan concerning HOW to solve your problem. You may ring Fred and explain that your friend will contact him today to prepare the ground and that you will meet him, if still necessary, in two days' time – when your car will be repaired. The picture gallery may have to wait.

However, your chosen solution may generate new problems which you will have to consider and solve. For example, IF your friend is not available to take your call you may have to take some other action – i.e., hire a car to get you to town X.

The process of thinking logically round the cycle, asking WHY?, WHAT?, HOW? and IF? questions, is the process of problem-solving as discussed in this book. We will see that some problems are more difficult to solve by purely logical means, and we will consider that point as well. However before we begin, we would like you to complete the Pre-assessment questionnaire. The first part is concerned with how you formally behave when faced with a problem; the second and third are attempts to determine your attitude to encouraging creativity in yourself and others.

Skill Pre-assessment

Diagnostic Surveys for Creative Problem-Solving

Problem-Solving, Creativity and Innovation

Instructions

Step 1: Before you read the material in this book, please respond to the following statements by writing a number from the rating scale below in the left-hand column (Pre-assessment). Your answers should reflect your attitudes and behaviour as they are now, not as you would like them to be. Be honest. This instrument is designed to help you discover your level of competency in problem-solving and creativity so you can tailor your learning to your specific needs. When you have completed the survey, use the Scoring Key at the end of the book (page 91) to identify the skills that are most important for you to master.

Step 2: After you have completed the reading and the exercises in this book, cover up your first set of answers and respond to the same statements again, this time in the right-hand column (Post-assessment). When you have completed the survey, go back to the Scoring Key at the end of the book (page 91) to measure your progress. If your score remains low in specific skill areas, use the behavioural guidelines at the end of the Skill Learning section to guide your further practice.

Rating Scale

6 Strongly agree	5 Agree	4 Slightly agree
3 Slightly disagree	2 Disagree	1 Strongly disagree

ASSESSMENT

PRE-	POST-	**When I approach a typical, routine problem**

_____ _____ 1. I always define clearly and explicitly what the problem is.

_____ _____ 2. I always generate more than one alternative solution to the problem.

_____ _____ 3. I evaluate the alternative solutions based on both long- and short-term consequences.

_____ _____ 4. I define the problem before solving it; that is, I avoid imposing my predetermined solutions on problems.

_____ _____ 5. I keep problem-solving steps distinct; that is, I make sure to separate formulating definitions, generating alternatives and finding solutions.

When faced with a complex or difficult problem that does not have a straight forward solution

_____ _____ 6. I try to define the problem in several different ways.

_____ _____ 7. I try to be flexible in the way I approach the problem; I don't just rely on conventional wisdom or past practice.

_____ _____ 8. I look for patterns or common elements in different aspects of the problem.

_____ _____ 9. I try to unfreeze my thinking by asking lots of questions about the nature of the problem.

_____ _____ 10. I try to apply both the left (logical) side of my brain and the right (intuitive) side of my brain to the problem.

_____ _____ 11. I frequently use metaphors or analogies to help me analyse the problem and discover what else it is like.

_____ _____ 12. I strive to look at problems from different perspectives so as to generate multiple definitions.

_____ _____ 13. I do not evaluate the merits of an alternative solution to the problem until I have generated other alternatives.

_____ _____ 14. I often break the problem down into smaller components and analyse each one separately.

_____ _____ 15. I strive to generate multiple creative solutions to problems.

When trying to foster more creativity and innovation among those with whom I work

_____ _____ 16. I help arrange opportunities for individuals to work on their ideas outside the constraints of normal procedures.

_____ _____ 17. I make sure there are divergent points of view represented in every problem-solving group.

_____ _____ 18. I sometimes make outrageous suggestions, even demands, to help stimulate people to find new ways of approaching problems.

_____ _____ 19. I try to acquire information from customers regarding their preferences and expectations.

_____ _____ 20. I sometimes involve outsiders (for example, customers or recognised experts) in problem-solving discussions.

_____ _____ 21. I provide recognition not only to those who are idea champions but also to those who support others' ideas and who provide resources to implement them.

_____ _____ 22. I encourage informed rule-breaking in pursuit of creative solutions.

How Creative Are You?

Introduction

The following test helps you determine if you have the personality traits, attitudes, values, motivations and interests that make up creativity. It is based on several years' study of attributes possessed by men and women in a variety of fields and occupations who think and act creatively.

Instructions

For each statement, write in the appropriate letter:

A = Agree   B = Undecided or Don't Know   C = Disagree

Be as frank as possible. Try not to second-guess how a creative person might respond[1]. The Scoring Key is towards the end of the book, page 92.

_____ 1. I always work with a great deal of certainty that I am following the correct procedure for solving a particular problem.

_____ 2. It would be a waste of time to ask questions if I had no hope of obtaining answers.

_____ 3. I concentrate harder than most people on whatever interests me.

_____ 4. I feel that a logical step-by-step method is best for solving problems.

[1]Liam Hudson, Contrary Imaginations, Penguin/Pelican (1966 and subsequent) showed that 'non-creatives' could enhance their apparent creativity by putting themselves into the role of someone they feel is creative. Hudson also found that the creative output of such people was inclined to be uncontrolled and uncensored by normal social conventions..

_____ 5. In groups I occasionally voice opinions that seem to turn some people off.

_____ 6. I spend a great deal of time thinking about what others think of me.

_____ 7. It is more important for me to do what I believe is right than to try to win the approval of others.

_____ 8. People who seem uncertain about things lose my respect.

_____ 9. More than other people, I need the things I take part in to be interesting and exciting.

_____ 10. I know how to keep my inner impulses in check.

_____ 11. I am able to stick with difficult problems over extended periods of time.

_____ 12. On occasion I get overly enthusiastic.

_____ 13. I often get my best ideas when doing nothing in particular.

_____ 14. I rely on intuitive hunches and the feeling of 'rightness' or 'wrongness' when moving toward the solution of a problem.

_____ 15. When problem solving, I work faster when analysing the problem and slower when synthesising the information I have gathered.

_____ 16. I sometimes enjoy breaking the rules and doing what I am not supposed to do.

_____ 17. I like hobbies that involve collecting things.

_____ 18. Daydreaming has provided the impetus for many of my more important projects.

_____ 19. I like people who are objective and rational.

_____ 20. If I had to choose from two occupations other than the one I now have, I would rather be a physician than an explorer.

_____ 21. I can get along more easily with people if they belong to the same social and business class as myself.

_____ 22. I have a high degree of aesthetic sensitivity.

_____ 23. I am driven to achieve high status and power in life.

_____ 24. I like people who are most sure of their conclusions.

_____ 25. Inspiration has nothing to do with the successful solution of problems.

_____ 26. When I am in an argument, my greatest pleasure would be for the person who disagrees with me to become a friend, even at the price of sacrificing my point of view.

_____ 27. I am much more interested in coming up with new ideas than in trying to sell them to others.

_____ 28. I would enjoy spending an entire day alone, just thinking.

_____ 29. I tend to avoid situations in which I might feel inferior.

_____ 30. In evaluating information, the source is more important to me than the content.

_____ 31. I resent things being uncertain and unpredictable.

_____ 32. I like people who follow the rule, 'business before pleasure'.

_____ 33. Self-respect is much more important than the respect of others.
_____ 34. I feel that people who strive for perfection are unwise.
_____ 35. I prefer to work with others in a team effort rather than solo.
_____ 36. I like work in which I must influence others.
_____ 37. Many problems I encounter cannot be resolved in terms of good or bad solutions.
_____ 38. It is important for me to have a place for everything and everything in its place.
_____ 39. Writers who use strange and unusual words merely want to show off.
_____ 40. Below is a list of terms that describe people. Choose ten words that best characterise you.

- formal
- informal
- dedicated
- forward-looking
- factual
- open-minded
- tactful
- inhibited
- enthusiastic
- innovative
- poised
- acquisitive
- practical
- quick
- good-natured
- thorough
- impulsive
- determined

- alert
- curious
- organised
- unemotional
- clear-thinking
- understanding
- dynamic
- self-demanding
- polished
- courageous
- efficient
- helpful
- perceptive
- sociable
- well-liked
- restless
- retiring
- realistic

- energetic
- persuasive
- observant
- fashionable
- self-confident
- persevering
- original
- cautious
- habit-bound
- resourceful
- egotistical
- independent
- stern
- predictable
- modest
- involved
- absent-minded
- flexible

(Source: Eugene Raudsepp, 1981)

Innovative Attitude Scale

Instructions

Please indicate how far each of the following statements are true of either your actual behaviour or your intentions at work. Use the following scale for your responses:

5 = Almost always true   4 = Often true   3 = Not applicable
2 = Seldom true   1 = Almost never true.

Use the Scoring Key at the end of the book (page 93) to interpret your answers.

_____   1. I discuss my progress and opportunities with my supervisor/boss.
_____   2. I try new ideas and approaches to problems.
_____   3. I take things or situations apart to find out how they work.
_____   4. I welcome uncertainty and unusual circumstances related to my tasks.
_____   5. I attempt to negotiate the conditions under which I work.
_____   6. I can be counted on to find a new use for existing methods or equipment.
_____   7. Among my colleagues and co-workers, I will be the first, or nearly the first, to try out a new idea or method.
_____   8. I take the opportunity to bring new information from other sources to my work group.
_____   9. I demonstrate originality.
_____ 10. I will work on a problem that has caused others great difficulty.
_____ 11. I provide an important role in developing a new solution.
_____ 12. I will provide well researched proposals of ideas to my work group.
_____ 13. I develop contacts with outside experts.
_____ 14. I will use influence to take on the parts of group projects I most enjoy.
_____ 15. I make time to pursue my own pet ideas or projects.
_____ 16. I set aside time and energies for the pursuit of risky ideas or projects.
_____ 17. I accept that rules may have to be broken to reach ideal solutions.
_____ 18. I speak out in group meetings.
_____ 19. I like working together to solve complex problems.
_____ 20. I see myself as sometimes providing light relief to others.

(Source: Etlie & O'Keefe, 1982)

Skill Learning

Problem-Solving, Creativity and Innovation

Problem-solving is a skill that is required of every person in virtually every aspect of life. Hardly an hour goes by without an individual having to solve some kind of problem. The job of the manager is inherently a problem-solving one. If there were no problems in organisations, there would be no need for managers. As a result, it is hard to conceive of an incompetent problem-solver succeeding as a manager.

In this book we offer specific guidelines and techniques for improving problem-solving skills. Two kinds of problem-solving are addressed – rational problem-solving and creative problem-solving. Effective managers are able to solve problems both rationally and creatively, even though different skills are required. Thamia and Woods (1984), reviewing 146 problem-solving sessions in the R&D department of a major European-based multinational, found that problem-solving techniques were used throughout the development process, and that a range of techniques – creative and rational – were applied with varying degrees of success. 32 per cent of the projects tackled over a three-year period were rational systems and 68 per cent were termed 'creative' systems. The success rate judged on an assessment by senior management some ten years later was approximately 60 per cent for creative problem-solving and about 80 per cent for rational systems. Geschka (1978), working with German industrial firms, gave figures for success of creative techniques of between 24 and 50 per cent.

Table 1 gives the split of the usage of techniques, both creative and rational, for the various stages of the development process.

Table 1

Stage of the innovation process	No of sessions – total 146	% of total sessions
Conception	42	29
Product/Process specification	12	8
Process engineer specification	19	13
Engineering/Production specification	32	22
Exploitation	12	18
Contingency planning	7	5
Clerical back-up	11	8
Completed commercial exploitation	11	8

(Source: Thamia and Woods, 1984)

In practice most managers begin the process of problem-solving with rational systems and only move reluctantly towards the creative mode (the data from Thamia and Woods in terms of the total problem-solving activity is obviously biased towards creative solutions since much of the rational problem-solving occurred informally before the work had been recorded). In spite of the reluctance on the part of many managers to think creatively, the ability to solve problems in the creative mode separates the sheep from the goats, career successes from career failures and achievers from derailed executives. It can also produce a dramatic impact on organisational effectiveness.

Therefore, the initial aim of this book is to increase the skills of individuals in fostering their own problem-solving techniques – rational and creative – and to help others improve their skills, particularly those for whom they have managerial responsibility. We see training and skill development in this area as a very large contribution towards the development of a learning organisation. Specific techniques (i.e., Thamia and Woods recorded 15 distinct types in their study) will be left to more specialised texts (Twiss, 1980; Buzan, 1974; Rickards, 1974, 1988).

Steps in Rational Problem-Solving

Most people, including managers, don't like problems – they are time-consuming and stressful. In fact, most people try to get rid of problems as soon as they can. Their natural tendency is to select the first reasonable solution that comes to mind (March & Simon, 1958), but these are rarely the best solutions. We often try to implement the marginally acceptable or satisfactory solution, as opposed to the optimal or ideal solution – a tendency in the West, that many observers claim to have been a major factor in the growth of the Japanese economy.

The most widely accepted model of rational problem-solving involves four steps, which are summarised in Table 2.

Table 2 A model of rational problem-solving

Step	Characteristics
1. Define the problem.	■ Identify the problem 'owner'. ■ State the problem explicitly. ■ Differentiate fact from opinion. ■ Specify underlying causes. ■ Tap everyone involved for information. ■ Identify what standard is being violated. ■ Separate the problem from the solution. ■ Define the constraints within which any potential solutions must operate ■ Define standards for potential solutions.
2. Generate alternative solutions.	■ Accept all the ideas that come – postpone evaluating alternatives. ■ If possible involve all the 'stakeholders'. ■ Keep to an 'agenda' – one problem at a time. ■ Specify both short- and long-term alternatives. ■ Build on your own and other's ideas.
3. Evaluate and select an alternative	■ Evaluate systematically. ■ Evaluate against standards within constraints. ■ Evaluate main effects and side effects. ■ State the selected alternative explicitly as a 'tentative solution' and look for what could go wrong before proceeding to implementation.

4. Implement and follow-up on the solution.
   - Plan ahead – starting, staging and resourcing.
   - Provide opportunities for feedback – listen.
   - Seek the acceptance of all those affected.
   - Establish an ongoing monitoring system.
   - Establish contingency plans for failure and be prepared to try again.

Step 1. Problem Definition

Problem definition involves diagnosing the situation so that the focus is on the real problem, not just on its symptoms. For example, suppose you have to deal with the problem of an employee who consistently fails to get his or her work done on time. Slow work might be the problem or it might only be a symptom of another underlying problem – i.e., bad health, low morale, lack of training or inadequate rewards. Defining the problem requires a wide search for information before any action is taken. The more relevant information that is acquired, the more likely it is that the problem will be defined accurately.

Good problem definition should have some of the following attributes:

1. Factual information is differentiated from opinion or speculation.
2. The constraints within which the solution needs to operate and the criteria – standards, against which any potential alternatives will be judged – are considered but put aside for the evaluation stage.

A number of engineers were asked to look at alternative feeding systems for fish farming. When the constraints and the standards were considered, the problem evaporated. It was necessary that one operator inspected each of the fish cages every day using a small boat. In addition, as safety regulations dictated that the operator needed a companion in case of trouble, it was fairly obvious that the companion might as well be feeding the fish as doing nothing.

3. As far as possible, everyone concerned with the problem is consulted.

We were asked to look into assaults on men delivering goods to certain deprived urban areas in UK. A whole range of solutions had been proposed, but surprisingly the delivery men themselves had not been consulted. Consultation not only provided a key to the solution but also helped the implementation since the people concerned had been involved.

4. The problem is stated explicitly. We find that the very process of writing a problem down imposes a discipline on the problem-holder that allows objectivity.

5. It is possible to think in terms of what was expected and what is happening.

Consultants were asked to look into labour turnover in an animal testing unit in a large laboratory. The concern was that the percentage of people leaving far exceeded the laboratory average. Looking closer at the figures the consultants found that like was not being compared with like – labour turnover figures being used were for the whole laboratory whose average age was 37 with 15% women in the population. Taking the animal handlers in isolation, the average age was 23 with 100% women. Taking a similarly composed sample in other industries, the turnover was below average.

6. The problem definition indicates whose problem it is.

For years, old people confined to residential care were separated by gender – a fact that often distressed many to whom this was not seen as a benefit. Looking at the 'problem' again, we see that there really is no problem since nobody loses by allowing life partners to stay together.

7. The definition is not simply a disguised solution: i.e., 'the problem is that we need to fire Henry because he is slow.' Interlocking the solution with the problem means that we will fail on all the attributes we have discussed and move directly to what will probably be inappropriate action.

A map is of no use unless you know where you are. Solving a problem without understanding what it is you have to solve is worse than useless, but is unfortunately a common practice.

Step 2. Generating Alternatives

The second step is to generate alternative solutions and this requires postponing the selection of one solution until several alternatives have been proposed. Delaying judgement as Gordon (1961) would put it, is an essential step in any form of effective problem solving. Maier (1970) found that the quality of the final solution can be significantly enhanced by considering multiple alternatives. Judgement and evaluation, therefore, must be postponed so the first acceptable solution suggested isn't the one that is immediately selected. As Broadwell (1972, p. 121) noted:

> The problem with evaluating [an alternative] too early is that we may rule out some good ideas by just not getting around to thinking about them. We hit on an idea that sounds good and we go with it, thereby never even thinking of alternatives that may be better in the long run.

As many alternatives as possible should be generated before evaluating any of them – poor alternatives often lead to good ones and without them quality solutions can often be missed.

> The problem given to a team was to de-bone a cooked chicken efficiently and quickly. One jokey solution was proposed whereby the chicken was 'blown up' using an explosive charge place in its body cavity: 'that would certainly take all the flesh off the bones'. The idea of blowing up the chicken, taken first as a joke, led to the use of rubber bags on stems inserted into the chickens and inflated so that the chickens could be held firmly. A sub-problem, found through consultation with people who worked on taking the flesh off cooked chickens, was that they were slippery to handle. The rubber bags on stems formed a sort of shoe maker's lasts that got over what proved to be the major problem.

A common problem in managerial decision making is that alternatives are evaluated as they are proposed, so the first acceptable (although frequently not optimal) one is chosen. If this had happened with the chicken example, a very practicable idea would have been lost. Good alternative-generation should have some of the following attributes:

1. The evaluation of each proposed alternative is postponed. (All alternatives should be proposed before evaluation is allowed.)
2. Alternatives are proposed by as many of the relevant individuals as possible – consider the 'delivery man example'.
3. The atmosphere during the process should be positive. Angry

or bitter people are unlikely to contribute much more than their discontent and may do actual harm by being given a platform.

4. The alternatives generated should cover both short- and long-term potential 'solutions' – the evaluation stage may well rule out ideas that do not meet the needs of the 'problem owner', but the generation stage is not the right place to make such judgement.

5. Alternatives should be allowed to build upon one another – bad ideas may become good ideas if combined with or modified by other ideas.

6. The 'agenda' is adhered to and alternatives are confined to potential solutions of the problem in hand. It is often interesting to go down new pathways, but should be avoided if it does not relate to the current problem.

The issue is one of credibility. In our experience very few organisations, with the notable exception of advertising agencies, find the process of problem-solving, and in particular problem-solving involving people from all over and even outside the organisation, a 'natural' activity. The presentation of half-baked, subversive or irrelevant ideas to mangers not involved in the seductive process of idea generation can be a very dangerous activity, and can seriously damage people's career prospects.

Step 3. Evaluating and Selecting Alternatives

The evaluation and selection step involves careful weighing up of the advantages and disadvantages of the proposed alternatives before making a final selection. In selecting the best alternative, skilled problem-solvers make sure that the alternatives are judged in terms of the extent to which:

- They meet the standards set for the 'solution' to the problem.
- They fit within the organisational constraints (e.g., it is consistent with policies, norms and budget limitations).
- All the individuals involved (especially the 'problem owner') will accept, and are happy to work with, the alternative suggested.

- Implementation of the alternative is likely.
- They will solve the problem without causing other unantici-
  pated problems.

Care is taken not to short-circuit these considerations by choosing
the most conspicuous alternative without considering others.
March and Simon (1958, p. 141) point out:

> Most human decision-making, whether individual or organisational, is
> concerned with the discovery and selection of satisfactory alternatives;
> only in exceptional cases is it concerned with the discovery and selec-
> tion of optimal alternatives. To optimise requires processes several
> orders of magnitude more complex than those required to satisfy. An
> example is the difference between searching a haystack to find the
> sharpest needle in it and searching the haystack to find a needle sharp
> enough to sew with.

Given the natural tendency to select the first satisfactory solution
proposed, the evaluation and selection step must not be underrated.

Good evaluation and selection should have some of the following attributes:

1. Alternatives are evaluated relative to a optimal standard rather
   than a satisfactory standard.
2. Evaluation of alternatives occurs systematically so each is given
   consideration. However, there are exceptions to this rule:

> We were asked to consider how to promote a food product, which in
> this case was a factory produced and very ordinary sausage. About ten
> minutes into the discussion someone suggested that the sausages
> should be promoted along with the inevitable mustard to be found on
> the British sausage eater's plate. The 'problem owner', the brand man-
> ager for the sausage product, leapt to his feet and rang up a friend in
> the company renowned for marketing British Mustard and arranged a
> deal. The session finished in disarray but a placard promoting the
> sausage AND the mustard appeared on bill boards within weeks.

If the problem owner is satisfied, it is pointless to demand a
structured approach to assessing ALL the ideas.

3. Alternatives are evaluated in terms of the goals of the organisation and the individuals involved. The implementation of ideas

needs both the support of the organisation and of the key individuals concerned.

We were asked to evaluate a concept for making quality envelopes for the domestic market, in a continuous process from a single strip of paper, the standard method being 'old fashioned'. The idea was fine and it met the criteria for new ideas laid out by the organisation. However, nobody in the organisation was happy enough with the idea to put his or her career on the line to implement it. The idea was dropped.

4. Alternatives are evaluated in terms of their effects in the wider world.

The Shell Company in 1995 evaluated various alternatives for the disposal of a redundant oil rig in the Atlantic. Logically, disposal at sea was the obvious choice – provided one did not predict the way in which environmentalists could exploit the issue to bring publicity against industrial pollution. However, Greenpeace chose to fight the decision and won, so that a precedent of what they saw as bad practice, was not established and the company had to back down from their 'logical' decision.

5. The alternative suggested is stated explicitly. We would suggest that a formal proposal is made with the reasoning behind the decision, including the case for and against both the chosen route and the non-recommended alternatives. We would see this as being the 'tentative solution' and that a meeting is called to find fault with the solution as proposed. Only then, when we are satisfied, would we proceed with the implementation stage. If we are not satisfied we would return either to select a different 'solution' or back to the problem definition stage.

Step 4. Implementing the Solution

The final step is to implement and follow-up on the solution. Implementation of any solution requires sensitivity to possible resistance from those who will be affected by it. Almost any change engenders some resistance. Therefore, the best problem-solvers are careful to select a strategy that maximises the probability that the solution will be accepted and fully implemented. This may involve ordering that the solution be implemented by others, 'selling' the solution to others or involving others in the implementation. Tannenbaum and Schmidt (1958), and Vroom and Yetton (1973) provide guidelines for managers to determine which of these implementation behaviours is most appropriate under which circumstances. Generally speaking, participation by others in the implementation of a solution will increase its acceptance and decrease resistance.

Effective implementation also requires some follow-up to check on implementation, prevent negative side-effects and ensure solution of the problem. Follow-up not only helps ensure effective implementation, but serves as a feedback function as well as providing information that can be used to improve future problem-solving. Drucker (1974, p. 480) explained:

> A feedback has to be built into the decision to provide continuous testing of the expectations that underlie the decision, against actual events. Few decisions work out the way they are intended to. Even the best decision usually runs into snags, unexpected obstacles and all kinds of surprises. Even the most effective decision eventually becomes obsolete. Unless there is feedback from the results of the decision, it is unlikely to produce the desired results.

Effective implementation and follow-up should include some of the following attributes:

1. Implementation occurs at the right time and in the proper sequence.
2. The implementation process includes opportunities for feedback. We need to be able to communicate how well the selected solution works.
3. Implementation is supported by the whole 'team', all of which should have been involved wherever and whenever possible in the process.
4. A system for monitoring the implementation process is set up with short-, medium- and long-term goals clearly laid out.
5. Evaluation of success is based on problem-solution, not on side-benefits. Although the solution may provide some positive

outcomes, unless it solves the problem being considered, it is unsuccessful.

Whatever is proposed we would suggest that contingency plans are set up. In any implementation process, problems will occur. Woods and Davies (1973), proposed a formal system between the assessment and implementation stages of structured problem-solving. They suggested that a team delegated with the implementation of a 'solution' of a problem were empowered to take all necessary actions for success. However, certain things were beyond the mandate of the team or individual and required higher authority. These they termed 'contingency actions'.

In the methodology they proposed, a 'Potential Problem Analysis' session would be conducted before the implementation stage – all likely snags in the implementation would be considered and solutions proposed. Residual problems, the problems likely to involve contingency work, would be listed at this point and referred to the problem owner for him or her to review what should be done, and indeed whether a complete rethink would be necessary.

> In the 1970s, many food companies were considering alternative processes for making animal-protein substitutes from various plant products. One source of such protein was derived from various pulses. Unfortunately several pulses, in the uncooked or semi-cooked state, contain a toxin which inhibits the human digestive system. The detoxification of the pulse material needed to be at the boiling point of water to be effective.
>
> During a Potential Problem Analysis session with the team responsible for the implementation, it was pointed out that the factory designated for the production of the product was likely to be at a height well above sea level and that open cooking might not detoxify the beans. The contingency plan would be to cook the beans in pressure vessels. Due consideration of the cost of the implementation of such pressure cooking led to a complete re-evaluation of the process and it being abandoned.

Thamia and Woods (1984) found seven examples of such contingency planning work in their studies.

Limitations of the Rational Problem-Solving Model

Most experienced problem-solvers are familiar with these steps in rational problem-solving, which are based on empirical research results and sound rationale (Kepner and Tregoe 1965; Maier, 1970; Huber, 1980; Elbing, 1978; Filley, House, & Kerr, 1976). Unfortunately, managers do not always practise them: the demands of the job often pressure managers into circumventing some of these steps, thus problem-solving suffers as a result. When these four steps are followed, however, effective problem-solving is markedly enhanced.

The research by Thamia & Woods records an incident where a senior manager in the multi-national studied, had been 'taught' the Kepner and Tregoe method on a course finishing on a Friday. On the next Monday he was in a senior management meeting where he proposed to use the technique to help making a significant decision. He was told: 'I know you have been on a course, but we simply do not have time for all that clap trap – what does everyone think we should do?'

On the other hand, simply learning about and practising the four steps of problem definition, alternative generation, evaluation and implementation does not guarantee that the individual will solve all problems effectively. There are two principle reasons for this.

Firstly, these problem-solving steps are useful mainly when the problems faced are straightforward, when alternatives are readily available, when relevant information is present, and when a clear standard exists against which to judge the correctness of a solution. Thompson and Tuden (1959) call problems with these characteristics 'computational problems', for which the main tasks are to gather information, generate alternatives and make an informed choice. The trouble is, many managerial problems are not of this type. Definitions, information, alternatives and standards are seldom unambiguous or readily available, so knowing the steps in problem-solving and being able to follow them are not the same thing.

Table 3 summarises our difficulties. Constraints, arising from individuals and the organisation make it difficult to follow any strict model.

Table 3 Some constraints on the rational problem-solving model

Steps	Constraints
1. Define the problem	■ There is seldom consensus as to the definition of the problem. ■ There is often uncertainty as to whose definition will be accepted. ■ Problems are usually defined in terms of the solutions already possessed.
2. Generate alternative solutions	■ Solution alternatives are usually evaluated one at a time as they are proposed. ■ Usually, few of the possible alternatives are known. ■ The first acceptable solution is usually accepted. ■ Alternatives are based on what was successful in the past.
3. Evaluate and select an alternative	■ Limited information about each alternative is usually available. ■ The search for information occurs close to home – in easily accessible places. ■ The type of information available is constrained by importance – primacy versus recency, extremity versus centrality, expected versus surprising, and correlation versus causation. ■ Gathering information on each alternative is costly. ■ The best alternative is not always known. ■ Satisfactory solutions, not optimal ones, are usually accepted. ■ Solutions are often selected by oversight or default.

	■ Solutions are often implemented before the problem is defined.
4. Implement and follow-up on the solution	■ Acceptance by others of the solution is not always forthcoming. ■ Resistance to change is a universal phenomenon. ■ It is not always clear what part of the solution should be monitored or measured in follow-up. ■ Political and organisational processes must be managed in any implementation effort. ■ It may take a long time to implement a solution.

A second reason why the rational problem-solving model is not always effective for managers concerns the nature of the problem itself. The problem may not be amenable to a systematic or rational analysis. In fact, for some problems, a rational problem-solving approach may not lead to an effective solution. Sufficient and accurate information may not be available, outcomes may not be predictable or the method of implementation may not be evident. In order to solve such problems, a new way of thinking may be required, multiple or conflicting definitions might be needed and alternatives never before considered may have to be generated; in short, creative problem-solving must be used.

Impediments to Creative Problem-Solving

Creative thinking involves three stages:
1. The destruction of the set patterns in our thought
2. An uncomfortable stage of insecurity while we establish new patterns
3. The re-establishment of new patterns.

It is a discomforting process and to avoid such discomfort most of us set up blocks – conceptual blocks – that defend the old patterns. It is these blocks that may make creative thought difficult.

Most of the time the presence of the blocks acts to defend us and helps us survive in a hugely complex and perhaps personally hostile world, but when we NEED to think creatively, they hold us back. Since the blocks are largely personal, as opposed to interpersonal or organisational, we need to develop skills to overcome them when it is appropriate.

Allen (1974) defined conceptual blocks as 'mental obstacles that constrain the way the problem is defined and limit the number of alternative solutions thought to be relevant'.

We all have and need conceptual blocks, but they are more numerous and more intense in some people than in others.

We need conceptual blocks because we are continuously bombarded with far more information than we can possibly handle, and they are part of our personal strategy to prevent information overload. Thus for example, most of us do not, if we are to remain sane, need to think about the mechanisms involved in us switching on an electric light. If we thought about it we would probably realise it is a fairly complex device connected by wires embedded in the plaster leading to a local distribution box, the box is itself connected . . . No, we simply turn on the light. Yet all of this information is available and is held by your brain. What we have done is to group the complexities into patterns and set them aside, noticing only the deviations from the patterns. By such grouping of things we can live in gross complexity and remain sane, focusing on events that do need our attention. The process of grouping and setting aside is the origin of our conceptual blocks. Though we may be unaware of the growth of the essential groupings into full conceptual blocks, the blocks prevent our taking on information that cannot be conveniently grouped and set aside. Consequently, the blocks can prevent us seeing, let alone solving some problems that require creative problem-solving.

Paradoxically, the more formal education individuals have, the more experience they have in a job, the less able they are to solve problems in creative ways. It has been estimated that most adults over 40 display less than two per cent of the creative problem-solving ability of a child under five. That's because formal education is about teaching how to group information and how to present the grouping to the satisfaction of all-knowing examiners – it works from 'right answers', analytic rules and thinking boundaries. Experience in a job teaches proper ways of doing things, specialised knowledge and rigid expectation of appropriate actions. Individuals lose the ability to experiment, improvise or take mental detours. Again, it is about grouping information to survive. Consider the following example:

> Place half a dozen bees and the same number of flies in a bottle, and lay it on its side, with its base to the window. The bees will persist, attempting to find a way through the glass of the base until they drop. The flies, moving at random, will soon find the neck of the bottle and escape. The bees' superior intelligence is the cause of their undoing. They appear to have learnt from past experience that the exit of EVERY prison is towards the brightest light, and they act accordingly. They persist on previous learning to their own destruction accepting that there is one right answer to escaping from confinement. In their persistence they ignore the new factor of the transparent barrier since they have no previous knowledge or experience of it and they do not have the adaptability to handle the new information. The less intelligent flies, with no such learning ability, ignore the call of the light and move at random until, suddenly, they are free. There is no one right answer because circumstances are always different.

This illustration identifies a paradox inherent in learning to solve problems creatively. On the one hand, more education and experience may inhibit creative problem-solving and reinforce conceptual blocks. As bees, individuals may not find solutions because the problem requires less 'educated' or more seemingly playful approaches. On the other hand, as several researchers have found, training directed toward improving thinking significantly enhances creative problem-solving abilities and managerial effectiveness (Barron, 1963; Taylor & Barron, 1963; Torrance, 1965).

A resolution to this paradox is not just more exposure to information or education; it is rather to focus on the process of thinking about certain problems in a creative way. As John Gardner (1965, p. 21) stated, it is learning to use the mind rather than merely filling it up:

All too often we are giving our young people cut flowers when we should be teaching them to grow plants. We are stuffing their heads with the products of earlier innovation rather than teaching them to innovate. We think of the mind as a storehouse to be filled when we should be thinking of it as an instrument to be used.

Parnes (1962), for example, found that training in thinking increased the number of good ideas produced in problem-solving by 125 per cent. Bower (1965) recorded numerous examples of organisations that increased profitability and efficiency through training in the improvement of thinking skills. Most large organisations send their managers to creativity workshops in order to improve their creative-thinking abilities.

Potters-Ballotini, an American owned company operating in the UK, had two factories turning glass waste into beads – the sizes of the beads ranged from close to dust for glitter in Christmas Cards to quite large marbles used to de-burr stone and metals.

The company's top six managers sat down together for a creative problem-solving session. No idea for a new use of the beads was rejected and some 100 ideas collected. One idea – that of incorporating the beads into a reflective paint for road marking – won through and has provided the company with an obvious and visible success ever since.

Problems Requiring a Creative Input

Some problems require creative rather than rational solutions. These are problems for which no acceptable alternative seems to be available, all reasonable solutions seem to be blocked or no obvious best answer is accessible. Handy (1994) tells the following story.

He was travelling in Ireland and looking for a particular place in the Wicklow hills. He stopped to ask a local who gave him accurate directions involving going up a steep hill until he got to Dave's Bar – 'When you get to the bar, you have passed it.'

DeBono (1971) gives a similar analogy of passing a turning and explains that creative thinking is like the reverse gear on a car. 'You do not need it all the time, but when you do, you better be able to use it.'

Something happens that makes a rational approach ineffective – we find ourselves in a useless Dave's Bar or in a cul-de-sac – we need to move into a creative problem-solving mode.

Two examples help illustrate the kinds of problems that require creative problem-solving skill. They illustrate several conceptual blocks that inhibit problem-solving and several techniques and tools that can be used to overcome them. We will refer to these examples several times in the remainder of this book.

Percy Spencer's and the Magnetron

During World War II Sir John Randall and Harry Boot, working on improving radar for the British Admiralty, developed a device they called the Cavity Magnetron. Radar systems using the Cavity Magnetron allowed aeroplanes to 'see' the surface of the earth and the sea. Apart from improving the offensive nature of the bomber, the device made it possible to detect and destroy submarines on the surface at great distances and was significant in winning what was called the Battle of the Atlantic. The original development, one of the closest secrets of World War ll, was completed for £200 on a laboratory bench but when Sir John Cockcroft took it across the Atlantic in 1940, it was considered to be one of the most valuable cargoes ever to sail.

Raytheon was one of several US firms invited to produce magnetrons for World War II. The workings of a magnetron were not well understood, even by sophisticated physicists and among the firms that made them; few understood what made the device work. A magnetron was tested, in those early days, by holding a neon tube next to it. If the neon tube got bright enough, the magnetron tube passed the test. In the process of conducting the test, the hands of the scientist holding the neon tube got warm. It was this phenomenon that led to a major creative breakthrough that eventually transformed lifestyles throughout the world.

At the end of the war, the market for radar essentially dried up and most firms stopped producing magnetrons. In Raytheon, however, a scientist named Percy Spencer had been experimenting with magnetrons, trying to think of alternative uses for the devices. He was convinced that magnetrons could be used to cook food by using the heat produced in the neon tube. The problem was, Raytheon was in the defence business – cooking devices seemed odd and out of place. Spencer was convinced that Raytheon should continue to produce magnetrons, even though production costs were prohibitively high. But Raytheon had lost money on the devices, and now there was no available market for magnetrons. The consumer product Spencer had in mind did not fit within the bounds of Raytheon's business.

As it turned out, Percy Spencer's solution to Raytheon's problem produced the microwave oven and a revolution in the cooking methods.

Further on, we will analyse several of the problem-solving techniques that are illustrated by his creative triumph.

Spence Silver's Glue

A second example of creative problem-solving began with Spence Silver's assignment to work on a temporary project team within the 3M company. The team was searching for new adhesives, so Silver obtained some material from AMD, Inc., which had potential for a new polymer-based adhesive. He described one of his experiments in this way: 'In the course of this exploration, I tried an experiment with one of the monomers in which I wanted to see what would happen if I put a lot of it into the reaction mixture. Before, we had used amounts that would correspond to conventional wisdom' (Nayak & Ketteringham, 1986). The result was a substance that failed all the conventional 3M tests for adhesives. It didn't stick. It preferred its own molecules to the molecules of any other substance. It was more cohesive than adhesive. It sort of hung around without making a commitment – it was a 'now-it-works, now-it-doesn't' kind of glue.

For five years Silver went from department to department within the company trying to find someone interested in using his newly found substance in a product. Silver had found a solution; he just couldn't find a problem to solve with it. Predictably, 3M showed little interest. The company's mission was to make adhesives that adhered ever more tightly. The ultimate adhesive was one that formed an unbreakable bond, not one that formed a temporary bond.

After four years the task force was disbanded and the team members assigned to other projects. But Silver was still convinced that his substance was good for something. He just didn't know what. As it turned out, Silver's solution has become the prototype for innovation in American firms and has spawned a half-billion dollars in annual revenues for 3M in a unique product called Post-It Notes.

These two examples are positive illustrations of how solving a problem in a unique way can lead to phenomenal business success. Creative problem-solving can have remarkable effects on both individuals' careers and on business success. To understand how to solve problems creatively, however, we must first reveal the blocks that inhibit this approach.

Conceptual Blocks

Table 4 summarises four types of conceptual blocks that inhibit creative problem-solving. Each is discussed and illustrated below with problems or exercises. We encourage you to complete the exercises and to solve the problems as you read the book because doing so will help you become aware of your own conceptual blocks. Later we shall discuss in more detail how you can over-come them.

Table 4 Conceptual blocks that inhibit creative problem-solving

1. CONSISTENCY

Vertical thinking	Defining a problem in only one way without considering alternative views.
One thinking language	Not using more than one means to define and assess the problem.

2. COMMITMENT

Stereotyping based on past experience	Present problems are seen only as variations of past problems.
Ignoring commonalties	Failing to perceive commonalities among elements that initially appear to be different.

3. COMPRESSION

Artificial constraints

Defining the boundaries of a problem too narrowly.

Distinguishing figure from ground

Not filtering out irrelevant information or finding needed information.

4. COMPLACENCY

Non-inquisitiveness

Not asking questions.

Non thinking

A bias toward activity in place of mental work.

Consistency

Consistency involves an individual becoming wedded to one way of looking at a problem or to one approach of defining, describing or solving it. Consistency is a valued attribute for most of us, most of the time. We like to appear at least moderately consistent in our approach to life, and consistency is often associated with maturity, honesty and even intelligence. We judge lack of consistency as untrustworthy, peculiar or erratic. Several prominent psychologists theorise, in fact, that a need for consistency is the primary motivator of human behaviour (Festinger, 1957; Heider, 1946; Newcomb, 1954). Many psychological studies have shown that once individuals take a stand or employ a particular approach to a problem, they are highly likely to pursue that same course without deviation in the future (see Cialdini, 1988, for multiple examples).

While consistency is a virtue when we are pursuing the correct course of action, it can be a fault when we are not and an alternative action would be better. Digging a different hole may well be better than digging the same hole deeper, faster or more cheaply. We can describe the block of consistency in terms of two ways of thinking – 'vertical' thinking and thinking confined to one 'language'. We will now explain these two terms.

Vertical Thinking

The terms 'vertical thinking', and its converse, 'lateral thinking', were coined by Edward deBono (1968). In vertical thinking, a problem is defined in a single way and then that definition is pursued without deviation until a solution is reached – no alternative definitions are considered. All information gathered and all alternatives generated are consistent with the original definition. In a search for oil, for example, vertical thinkers determine a spot for the hole and drill the hole deeper and deeper hoping to strike oil. Instead of drilling one hole deeper and deeper, lateral thinkers would drill a number of holes in different places in search of oil.

The vertical-thinking conceptual block arises from not being able to view the problem from multiple perspectives. Returning to our hole metaphor, we see that we are getting less and less advantage from the hole we have begun and stand aside to think that new holes, or even a tunnel, might be preferred. When faced with a problem, lateral thinkers generate alternative ways of viewing a problem and produce multiple definitions.

> Mechanical cod fish processing in Britain and Germany had been developed from the highly skilled craftsmanship of the fish filleter. The filleter had to prepare neat fillets to be attractive for sale from fishmongers slabs. As more and more cod fish were sent directly to factories to be made into frozen shaped fish pieces, the craftsmanship of the filleter was mechanised and refined. Nobody asked: ' Why do we need perfect fillets when there is no fishmongers slab to exhibit them?'
>
> Once the question had been asked, Nordsee in Germany and the Unilever company, Birds Eye in UK, came up with a range of new processes where the fish went directly into the process with no intermediate step of the perfect fillet.

What has happened is that the problem-solver has changed the definition of the problem from: How do we improve the manufacture of fish fillets?, to 'How do we get skinless and boneless fish flesh in a form acceptable to a processing plant from whole fish?'

Plenty of examples exist of creative solutions that have occurred because an individual refused to get stuck with a single problem definition. Alexander Graham Bell was trying to devise a hearing aid when he shifted definitions and invented the phonograph. Colonel Sanders was trying to sell his recipe to restaurants when he shifted definitions and developed his Kentucky Fried Chicken business. Karl Jansky was studying telephone static when he shifted definitions, discovered radio waves from the Milky Way galaxy, and developed the science of radio astronomy.

In the development of the microwave industry described earlier, Percy Spencer shifted the definition of the problem from 'How can we save our military radar business at the end of the war?' to 'What other applications can be made for the magnetron?' Other problem definitions followed, such as 'How can we make magnetrons cheaper?', 'How can we mass-produce magnetrons?', 'How can we convince someone besides the military to buy magnetrons?', 'How can we enter a consumer products market?', 'How can we make microwave ovens practical and safe?' And so on. Each new problem definition led to new ways of thinking about the problem, new alternative approaches, and eventually, to a new microwave oven industry.

Spence Silver at 3M is another example of someone who changed problem-definitions. He began with 'How can I get an adhesive that has a stronger bond?', but switched to 'How can I find an application for an adhesive that doesn't stick?' Eventually, other problem definitions followed such as, 'How can we get this new glue to stick to one surface but not another (e.g., to note-paper but not normal paper)?', 'How can we replace staples, drawing pins and paper clips in the workplace?', 'How can we manufacture and package a product that uses non-adhesive glue?', 'How can we get anyone to pay $1. 00 for a pad of scrap paper?' And so on.

Shifting definitions is not easy, of course, because it is not normal behaviour. It requires that individuals deflect their tendencies toward constancy. Later we will discuss some hints and tools that can help overcome the constancy block while avoiding the negative consequences of being inconsistent.

A Single Thinking Language

A second manifestation of the constancy block is the use of only one thinking language. Most people faced with a problem attempt to express it in words – spoken or written. The problem is that words almost always carry images with them.

Working with training groups in Unilever, Mike Woods and George Davies used to say that they were wishing to design a new garden 'truck' – a wheelbarrow. They would then ask the group members to describe what he of she saw when the word wheelbarrow was mentioned. Almost always, under questioning, the participant would be able to describe the wheelbarrow in detail; its colour, age, scars and even where it was – 'propped up against the wall of a garden shed'. The word wheelbarrow produced a complete image, so any new design of the wheelbarrow needed to compete against that total image before it was accepted as an viable concept. Thus if a new concept for a garden 'truck' was called a wheelbarrow and it would not park easily against a particular garden shed, it might well be rejected.

To confirm this, the groups were presented with a new concept 'wheelbarrow' and asked to write down the first comment that came into their heads. 80 per cent of the comments were negative – comments related to the fact that the word 'wheelbarrow' conjured up the image of a very detailed status quo to be challenged by the concept.

Rational problem-solving reinforces the use of words and the subsequent dangers. Some writers, in fact, have argued that thinking cannot even occur without words (Vygotsky, 1962). However, other thought languages are available, such as non-verbal or symbolic languages (e.g., mathematics), sensory imagery (e.g., smelling or tactile sensation), feelings and emotions (e.g., happiness, fear or anger), and visual imagery (e.g., mental pictures). The more languages available to problem-solvers, the better and more creative will be their solutions. As Koestler (1967) puts it, '[Verbal] language can become a screen which stands between the thinker and reality. This is the reason that true creativity often starts where [verbal] language ends.' Percy Spencer at Raytheon is a prime example of a visual thinker:

> One day, while Spencer was lunching with Dr. Ivan Getting and several other Raytheon scientists, a mathematical question arose. Several men, in a familiar reflex, pulled out their slide rules, but before any could complete the equation, Spencer gave the answer. Dr. Getting was astonished. 'How did you do that?' he asked. 'The root,' said Spencer shortly. 'I learned cube roots and squares by using blocks as a boy. Since then, all I have to do is visualise them placed together.' (Scott, 1974, p. 287).

The microwave oven not only depended on Spencer's command of multiple thinking languages, but it would never have got off the ground without a critical incident that illustrates the power of visual thinking. By 1965, Raytheon was just about to give up on any consumer application of the magnetron when a meeting was held with George Foerstner, the president of the recently acquired Amana Refrigeration Company. In the meeting, costs, applications, manufacturing obstacles and so on were discussed. Foerstner galvanised the entire microwave oven effort with the following statement, as reported by a Raytheon vice president.

> George says, 'It's no problem. It's about the same size as an air conditioner. It weighs about the same. It should sell for the same. So we'll price it at $499.' Now you think that's silly, but you stop and think about it. Here's a man who really didn't understand the technologies. But there is about the same amount of copper involved, the same amount of steel as an air conditioner. And these are basic raw materials. It didn't make a lot of difference how you fitted them together to make them work. They're both boxes; they're both made out of sheet metal; and they both require some sort of trim. (Nayak & Ketteringham, 1986, p. 181).

In short sentences Foerstner had taken one of the most complicated military secrets of World War II and translated it into something no more complex than a room air conditioner. He had painted a picture of an application that no one else had been able to capture by describing a magnetron visually, as a familiar object, not as a set of calculations, formulas or blueprints.

A similar occurrence in the Post-It Note chronology also led to a breakthrough. Spence Silver had been trying for years to get someone in 3M to adopt his un-sticky glue. Art Fry, another scientist with 3M, had heard Silver's presentations before. One day while singing in Church, Fry was fumbling around with the slips of paper that marked the various hymns in his book. Suddenly, a visual image popped into his mind.

> 'I thought, gee! If I had a little adhesive on these bookmarks, that would be just the ticket. So I decided to check into that idea the next week at work. What I had in mind was Silver's adhesive .... I knew I had a much bigger discovery than that. I also now realised that the primary application for Silver's adhesive was not to put it on a fixed

surface like the bulletin boards. That was a secondary application. The primary application concerned paper to paper. I realised that immediately' (Nayak & Ketteringham, 1986, p. 63–4).

Years of verbal descriptions had not led to any application for Silver's glue. Tactile thinking (handling the glue) has also failed. However, thinking about the product in visual terms, as applied to what Fry initially called 'a better bookmark', led to the breakthrough.

This emphasis on using alternative thinking languages, especially visual thinking, is now becoming the new frontier in scientific research. With the advent of super-computers, scientists are more and more working with pictures and simulated images rather than with numerical data. 'Scientists who are using the new computer graphics say that by viewing images instead of numbers, a fundamental change in the way researchers think and work is occurring. People have a lot easier time getting an intuition from pictures than they do from numbers and tables of formulas. In most physics experiments, the answer used to be a number or a string of numbers. In the last few years the answer has increasingly become a picture.' (Markoff, 1988, p. D3)

To illustrate the differences among thinking languages, consider the following two simple problems.

1. Below is the Roman numeral 9. By adding only a single line, turn it into a 6.

IX

2. Figure 1 shows seven match-sticks. By moving only one match-stick, make the figure into a true equality (i.e., the value on one side equals the value on the other side). Before looking up the answers at the end of the book (page 94), try defining the problems differently, and try using different thinking languages. How many answers can you find?

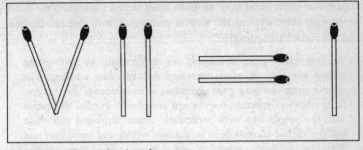

FIGURE 1   The matchstick configuration

Commitment

Commitment can also serve as a conceptual block to creative problem-solving.

Many local government-owned house estates throughout Europe suffer from neglect and vandalism. A process whereby the houses are sold to the tenants is increasing – the political issues are not our concern. The concern is that many of the problems of disrepair vanish with ownership. Where previously the local government official was blamed for not repairing the gutter or painting the window and nothing was done, now with ownership the ladders appear and the paint pots are emptied. Commitment by ownership works.

A host of other studies have demonstrated the same phenomenon. However, commitment is not always a positive effect, it may well be its own conceptual block.

Stereotyping Based on Past Experience – Defending the Status Quo

March and Simon (1958) point out that a major obstacle to innovative problem-solving is that individuals tend to define present problems in terms of problems they have faced in the past. Current problems are usually seen as variations on some past situation, so the alternatives proposed to solve the current problem are ones that have proved to be successful in the past. Both problem definition and proposed solution are therefore restricted by past experience. This restriction is referred to as 'perceptual stereotyping' (Allen, 1974). That is, certain preconceptions formed on the basis of past experience determine how an individual defines a situation. With perceptual stereotyping the new is compared with the established and dismissed accordingly.

> Working with a group developing new ready meals, we were testing various concepts including roast beef and Yorkshire pudding. The sample group showed a great divergence in acceptance of the concept, some members rejecting the concept completely. Further discussion with the people who were particularly dismissive found that these individuals had recently been in military service and 'roast beef and Yorkshire pudding' consisted of very thin over-cooked meat and biscuit-consistency Yorkshire pudding. The very words 'roast beef and Yorkshire pudding' conjured up a very unhappy experience in their lives and they reacted accordingly.

When individuals receive an initial cue regarding the definition of a problem, all subsequent problems may be framed in terms of that initial cue. There are advantages in this, perceptual stereotyping helps organise problems on the basis of a limited amount of data, and the need to consciously analyse every problem encountered is eliminated. On the other hand, perceptual stereotyping prevents individuals from viewing a problem in novel ways.

Both the creation of microwave ovens and that of Post-It Notes provide examples of overcoming stereotyping based on past experiences. Scott (1974) described the first meeting of Sir John Cockcroft, the technical leader of the British radar system that invented magnetrons, and Percy Spencer of Raytheon as follows:

> Cockcroft liked Spencer at once. He showed him the magnetron and the American regarded it thoughtfully. He asked questions – very intelligent ones – about how it was produced and the British scientist answered at length. Later Spencer wrote, 'The technique of making these tubes, as described to us, was awkward and impractical.' Awkward and impractical! Nobody else dared draw such a judgement about a product of undoubted scientific brilliance, produced and displayed by the leaders of British science.

Despite his admiration for Cockcroft and the magnificent magnetron, Spencer refused to abandon his curious and inquisitive stance. Rather than following the example of other scientists and assuming that since the British invented it and were using it, they surely knew how to produce a magnetron, Spencer broke out of the stereotypes and pushed for improvements.

Similarly, Spence Silver at 3M described his invention in terms of breaking stereotypes based on past experience.

> 'The key to the Post-It adhesive was doing the experiment. If I had sat down and factored it out beforehand, and thought about it, I wouldn't have done the experiment. If I had really seriously cracked the books and gone through the literature, I would have stopped. The literature was full of examples that said you can't do this (Nayak & Ketteringham, 1986, p. 57).'

This is not to say that one should avoid learning from past experience or that failing to learn the mistakes of history does not doom us to repeat them. Rather, it is to say that commitment to a course of action based on past experience can inhibit viewing problems in new ways, and it can even inhibit us from being able to solve some problems at all.

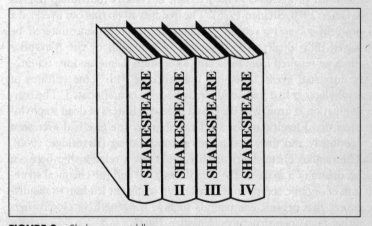

FIGURE 2 Shakespeare riddle

(Source: Raudsepp & Hough, 1977)

In Figure 2, there are four volumes of Shakespeare on the shelf. The pages of each volume are exactly two inches thick and the covers are each one-sixth of an inch thick. A bookworm started eating at page 1 of Volume I and ate straight through to the last page of Volume IV. What is the distance the worm covered? (The answer can be found in the Scoring Key section at the end of the book, page 94.) Solving this problem is relatively simple, but it requires that you overcome a stereotyping block to get the correct answer. (A clue – we find the problem virtually impossible unless we can work with real books – we need to touch and try before we get to the correct answer. We need to move to a different language.)

Ignoring Commonalties

A second manifestation of the commitment block is failure to identify similarities among seemingly disparate pieces of data. This is among the most commonly identified blocks to creativity. It means that a person becomes committed to a particular point of view, to the fact that elements are different, and becomes unable to make connections, identify themes or to perceive commonalties.

The ability to find one definition or solution for two seemingly dissimilar problems is a characteristic of creative individuals (Dellas & Gaier, 1970; Steiner, 1978). The inability to do this can overload a problem-solver by requiring that every problem encountered be solved individually. The discovery of penicillin by Sir Alexander Fleming resulted from his seeing a common theme among seemingly unrelated events. Fleming was working with some cultures of staphylococci that had accidentally become contaminated. The contamination, a growth of fungi and isolated clusters of dead staphylococci, led Fleming to see a relationship no one else had ever seen previously and thus to discover a wonder drug (Beveridge, 1960). The famous chemist Friedrich Kekule saw a relationship between his dream of a snake swallowing its own tail and the chemical structure of organic compounds. This creative insight led him to the discovery that organic compounds such as benzene have closed rings rather than open structures (Koestler, 1967).

For Percy Spencer at Raytheon, seeing a connection between the heat of a neon tube and the heat required to cook food was the creative connection that led to his breakthrough in the microwave industry. One of Spencer's colleagues recalled: 'In the process of testing a bulb [with a magnetron], your hands got hot. I don't know when Percy really came up with the thought of microwave ovens, but he knew at that time – and that was 1942. He [remarked] frequently that this would be a good device for cooking food.' Another colleague described Spencer this way: 'The way Percy Spencer's mind worked is an interesting thing. He had a mind that allowed him to hold an extraordinary array of associations on phenomena and relate them to one another.' (Nayak & Ketteringham, 1986, p. 184, 205). Similarly, the connection Art Fry made between a glue that wouldn't stick tightly and marking hymns in a choir book was the final breakthrough that led to the development of the revolutionary Post-It Note business.

To test your own ability to see commonalties, answer the following three questions:

1. What are some common terms that apply to both water and finance?
2. What is humorous about the following story: 'Descartes, the philosopher, walked into a university class. Recognising him, the instructor asked if he would like to lecture. Descartes replied, 'I think not,' and promptly disappeared.'
3. What does the single piece of wood look like that will pass through each hole in the transparent block in Figure 3, but that will touch all sides as it passes through? Answers can be found in the Scoring Key at the end of the book (pages 94–95).

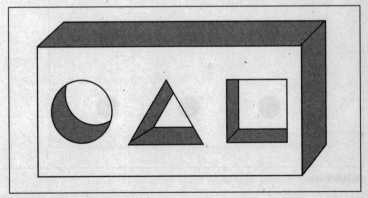

FIGURE 3 A block problem

(Source: McKim, 1972)

Compression

Conceptual blocks also occur as a result of compression of ideas – looking too narrowly at a problem, screening out too much relevant data, or making assumptions that inhibit problem-solution, are common examples.

Artificial Constraints

Sometimes people place boundaries around problems, or constrain their approach to them, in such a way that the problems become impossible to solve. Such constraints arise from hidden assumptions people make about problems they encounter. People assume that some problem definitions or alternative solutions are out of bounds – somehow cheating, and they ignore them. For an illustration of this conceptual block, look at Figure 4a. Without lifting your pencil from the paper, draw four straight lines that pass through all nine dots. Complete the task before reading further.

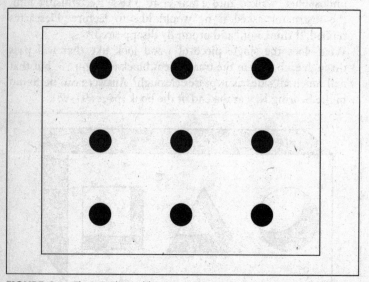

FIGURE 4a   The nine-dot problem

By thinking of the figure as more constrained than it actually is, the problem becomes impossible to solve. To solve the problem we have to MOVE OUTSIDE THE SQUARE. The assumption we make is that we have to stay 'joining the dots' without moving outside the square – this somewhat cheating.

Now 'cheat' some more – move further out on the assumptions that you have set for yourself when you saw the problem – join the dots with three lines and try it with one line. Can you determine how to put a single straight line through all nine dots without lifting your pencil from the paper? (Some rather exotic answers are given in the Scoring Key at the end of the book, page 95.)

Artificially constraining problems means simply that the problem-definition and the possible alternatives are limited more than the problem requires. Creative problem-solving requires that individuals become adept at recognising their hidden assumptions and expanding the alternatives they consider – or using the metaphor MOVING OUTSIDE THE SQUARE (see Figure 4b).

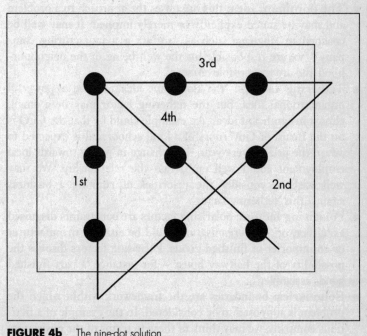

FIGURE 4b   The nine-dot solution

A British based textile company found itself faced with very strong opposition from the Far East and reduced sales. The large sales force was spurred on to work much harder and make more visits, but the situation only got worse and profitability fell still further. 'Moving outside the square' with the management team it was found that the problem was that marginal sales to an increased number of customers was actually costing the company money, and that in the rush for sales at any price the sales staff were offering a diversity of products that made the manufacturing division operate at a loss. **The solution was not more visits but less.** Marginal customers were gently recommended to shop with competitors, and focused meetings with valued volume customers were set up.

Edward deBono (1971) explains a technique for 'moving outside the square' and looking at the constraints that define a problem. He sees the constraints around a situation as being defined by five factors:

- **The dominant idea:** this organises the approach to a problem and may be stated explicitly or merely implied. It may well be coached in language such as, 'we are a manufacturing company', 'we are responsible for the well-being of the neighbourhood and are responsible citizens'.
- **Tethering factors:** 'the dominant idea may be a powerful organisational idea, but the tethering factor may be a small, almost insignificant idea.' An example could be that the CEO is on the Board of Governors of a local school and is expected to award the prizes every year. Any change in policy towards local employment could well embarrass the relationship. We may well wish to consider the priorities of running a business against this 'tethering factor'.
- **Polarising factors:** polarising factors are constraints disguised as 'either, or'. An organisation could be either a manufacturer or an importer of finished goods. Polarising factors dismiss the possibility of the halfway house – for instance 'a part-finished goods assembler'.
- **Boundaries:** boundaries are the framework within which the problem is supposed to be considered. In the example of a fictitious company, we may think of these in terms of the position of

the shareholders or the bank – 'we have to live within the constraints set by the bank', 'the shareholders have bought into a UK based company'. The statement may be true but check it!

■ **Assumptions**: boundaries are the limits of the ideas and assumptions are the building blocks that created the boundaries. We assume that the bank is not open to negotiation and that the shareholders will not be open to reasoned argument.

Using a non-judgement questioning of the five factors we can redesign the problem creatively and have a chance of reaching new solutions.

DeBono concludes that it is never possible to examine all the constraints, but that in setting them out to look for them logically, one becomes aware of the cage within which one is operating. Thus it is possible to consider whether this particular cage is relevant for the present time and place.

The Ford Motor Company 'EQUIP' programme for training and developing engineers in Europe insists that assumptions are recorded and shared before meetings. The agenda of the meeting is circulated in advance and nothing is discussed before the sharing is completed. Thus, they might be discussing safety bags in small cars and the pooled assumptions might include:

■ Too bulky for the current small cars range.
■ European drivers would not want it.
■ Difficult to make reliable at a price.

Any of the assumptions, if not tabled BEFORE the discussion could well encourage the individual holding the assumption to act negatively or even sabotage the discussion. Tabled, they can be seen for what they are – assumptions capable of challenge.

Seeing the Wood from the Trees
Questioning constraints in the way that deBono suggests will not always lead to solutions. Sometimes it is the lack of clear constraints that prevents clear thought. Problems almost never come clearly specified, so problem-solvers must determine what the real problem is. They must filter out inaccurate, misleading or

irrelevant information in order to correctly define the problem and to generate appropriate alternative solutions. The inability to separate the important from the unimportant, to appropriately compress problems, serves as a conceptual block because it exaggerates the complexity of the problem and inhibits a simple definition.

How easy is it for you to filter out irrelevant information? Consider Figure 5. For each pair, find the pattern on the left that is embedded in the more complex pattern on the right. On the complex pattern, outline the embedded pattern. Now try to find at least two figures in each pattern. (Our solution is given at the end of the book in the Scoring Key section, page 96.)

The compression block – seeing the wood from the trees, and artificially constraining problems – were important factors in the microwave oven and the Post-It Note breakthroughs. George Foerstner's contribution to the development and manufacture of the microwave oven was directly a product of his ability to compress the problem, that is, to separate out all the irrelevant complexity that constrained others. Whereas the magnetron was a device so complicated that few people understood it, Foerstner focused on its basic raw materials, its size and its functionality. By comparing it to an air conditioner, he eliminated much of the complexity and mystery, and, as described by two analysts, 'he had seen what all the researchers had failed to see, and they knew he was right' (Nayak & Ketteringham, 1986, p. 181).

On the other hand, Spence Silver had to add complexity, to overcome compression, in order to find an application for his product. Because the glue had failed every traditional 3M test for adhesives, it was categorised as a useless configuration of chemicals. The potential for the product was artificially constrained by traditional assumptions about adhesives – more stickiness, stronger bonding – until Art Fry visualised some unconventional applications – a better bookmark, a bulletin board, a notepad, and, paradoxically, a replacement for 3M's main product, tape.

The issue of seeing the wood from the trees – refusing to accept the constraints implied by the question and the questioner – is an art and is the art practised by all good consultants.

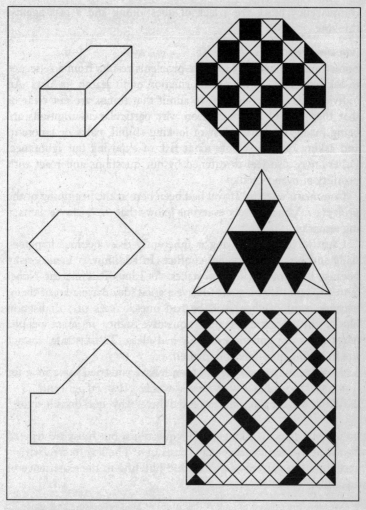

FIGURE 5 Embedded patterns

The Complacency Block

This occurs because of fear, ignorance, insecurity, or just plain mental laziness. Two especially prevalent examples of the complacency block are a lack of questioning and a bias against thinking.

Non-inquisitiveness

Sometimes the inability to solve problems results from a reticence to ask questions, to obtain information or to search for data. An individual is often reluctant to admit that things are not clear or that they do not see the reason why particular assumptions are being made. We have a fear of looking stupid, naive or ignorant, and asking questions puts us at risk of exposing our ignorance. Others may also feel threatened by our questions and react with hostility or even ridicule.

Comments such as 'If you had been here at the beginning of the project . . .', and 'Surely everyone knows that . . .', can be damaging remarks.

Creative problem-solving is inherently risky because it potentially involves interpersonal conflict. In addition, it is also risky because it is fraught with mistakes. As Linus Pauling, the Nobel laureate, said, 'If you want to have a good idea, have a lot of them, because most of them will be bad ones.' Years of socialisation blocks the adventurous and inquisitive stance in most people. Most of us are not rewarded for bad ideas. To illustrate, answer the following questions for yourself.

1. How many times in the last month have you tried something for which the probability of success was less than 50 per cent?
2. When was the last time you asked three 'why' questions in a row?

Children begin by asking WHY? questions, but most are trained by the age of ten to accept the status quo. The key to creativity is accepting the naiveté of a child and building in the experience of an adult.

> We were once asked to look at the future of food processing and chose to work with a small panel of six- to nine-year-olds. The kids were all from middle class families most of whom were concerned with the client company in some way.
>
> The first question we asked was – 'Does food go bad?'
>
> The answer was a resounding NO, but under pressure they admitted that milk occasionally went off – 'And Daddy makes it into cream

cheese, but Mummy throws it away when he is not looking.'

We then went on to ask why we put things into tins – baked beans for instance.

'Because if we didn't they would run all over the shelf', was the answer that came back.

We persisted. 'Does meat go bad?' 'NO'. 'NO never, we have some pigs behind our house running about and they don't go bad.'

Very easy to laugh but the questions for us, after the children had left, were 'Why does meat on the hoof not go bad?' and – 'Is life used as a method of preserving food anywhere in the world?' The answer to the last question is yes; many hot countries sell live animals in the market place for slaughter directly before preparation. The more adult question moves on to, 'What is different about life from death?' – a question we were not able to answer ourselves so we called in an expert enzymologist to help us. He explained that one way of looking at life and death is a battle fought by the enzymes of vitality and decay, with the decay processes winning once the brain ceases to referee the battle on the side of life. He explained that enzymes were used to 'tenderise' or accelerate the 'rotting' of meat by injection into live animals prior to slaughter and that there was no reason why they should not be used for the opposite purpose. We had a new line of research.

David Feldman (1988) lists more than 100 questions designed to shake complacency. For example:

- Why are people immune to their own body odour?
- Why are there twenty-one guns in a twenty-one-gun salute?
- What happens to the tread that wears off tyres?
- Why doesn't sugar spoil or get mouldy?
- Why doesn't a two-by-four measure two inches by four inches?
- Why doesn't postage-stamp glue have flavouring?
- Why is the telephone keypad arranged differently from that of a calculator?
- How do people who throw their hats in the air find them later?
- Why is Jack the nickname for John?
- How do they print 'M&M' on M&M sweets?

Tudor Rickards (1988) suggests that you should go about your work with a notebook and write down the things that annoy you, but about which you are too busy to do anything at the time. He suggests that you call them Puxxles. John Oakland (1994) working from the concept of Total Quality Management calls these problem items 'Snags' and advises managers to create a Snag list. The point of Puxxles and Snags is that by giving time and importance to the process of asking WHY? we provide opportunities for innovation.

> In a session on Puxxles in the University of Miskolc in Hungary in 1993, a group run by Mike Woods came up with five 'problems' in the spectacles that many of us wear. Why do:
> - The screws holding the frames come out?
> - The lenses fall out?
> - The lenses get scratched?
> - Long-sighted people always loose them?
> - They are a danger when they break?
>
> These problems can be seen as an opportunity for a design that has hardly changed since the days of Samuel Pepys in the 17th century.

Most of us are a little too complacent to even ask such questions, let alone to find out the answers! We often stop being inquisitive as we get older because we learn that it is good to be intelligent and being intelligent is interpreted as already knowing the answers (instead of asking good questions). Consequently, we learn less well at 35 than at five; we take fewer risks; we avoid asking why; and we function in the world without trying to understand it. Creative problem-solvers, on the other hand, are frequently engaged in inquisitive and experimental behaviour. Spence Silver at 3M described his attitude about the complacency block this way:

> 'People like myself get excited about looking for new properties in materials. I find that very satisfying, to perturb the structure slightly and just see what happens. I have a hard time talking people into doing that – people who are more highly trained. It's been my experience that people are reluctant just to try, to experiment – just to see what will happen' (Nayak & Ketteringham, 1986, p. 58).

Bias Against Thinking
A second demonstration of the complacency block is in an inclination to avoid doing mental work. This block, like most of the others, is a mixture of cultural and personal bias. For example,

assume that you passed by your assistant's office one day and noticed them leaning back in a chair, staring out the window. A half-hour later, as you passed by again, their position is the same. What would be your conclusion? Most of us would assume that no work was being done. We would assume that unless we saw action, our assistant was not being productive. However, they may well be THINKING.

When was the last time you heard someone say, 'I'm sorry. I can't go to the football (concert, dance, party or cinema) because I have to think?' or 'I'll do the dishes tonight. I know you need to catch up on your thinking?' The fact that these statements sound humorous illustrates the bias most people develop toward action rather than thought, or against putting their feet up, rocking back in their chair, looking off into space and engaging in solitary mental activity. This does not mean daydreaming or fantasising, but *thinking*.

There is a particular conceptual block in our culture against the kind of thinking that uses the right hemisphere of the brain. Left-hemisphere thinking, for most people, is concerned with logical, analytic, linear or sequential tasks. Thinking using the left hemisphere is apt to be organised, planned and precise, for example, language and mathematics are left-hemisphere activities.

Right-hemisphere thinking, on the other hand, is concerned with intuition, synthesis, playfulness and qualitative judgement. It tends to be more spontaneous, imaginative and emotional than left-hemisphere thinking. The emphasis in most formal education is toward left-hemisphere thought development. problem-solving on the basis of reason, logic and utility is generally rewarded, while problem-solving based on sentiment, intuition or pleasure is frequently considered tenuous and inferior.

A number of researchers have found that the most creative problem-solvers are ambidextrous in their thinking. That is, they can use both left- and right-hemisphere thinking and easily switch from one to the other (Bruner, 1966; Hermann, 1981; Martindale, 1975). Creative ideas arise most frequently in the right hemisphere but must be processed and interpreted by the left, so creative problem-solvers use both hemispheres equally well.

Try the exercise in Table 5, the idea of which came from von Oech (1986), and was developed by the authors of the work on Neuro Linguistic Programming by Bandler and Grindler (1979). It illustrates this ambidextrous principle. There are four lists of words. Take a minute to memorise the first list. Then, on a piece of paper write down as many as you can remember. Now memorise the words in each of the other three lists, one at a time taking a minute for each, writing down as many as you can remember.

Table 5   Exercise to test ambidextrous thinking

List 1	List 2	List 3	List 4
decline	sunset	fresh	bang
very	perfume	strawberries	swish
ambiguous	brick	sea breeze	alarm
resources	monkey	fresh baked	hear
term	castle	bread	silence
conceptual	guitar	fur	squeal
about	pencil	strike	ring
appendix	computer	hold	chord
determine	umbrella	solid	click
forget	radar	unhappy	interview
quantify	blister	firm	sing
survey	chessboard	gentle	out of tune
		handle	
		panicky	

Most people will have a 'favourite' list but few are most effective on the first list. The second list contains words that relate to visual perceptions, the third list relates to what Grindler and Bandler call 'kinesthetic' sensations, and the fourth list relates to the auditory senses. Your preference relates to the way in which you prefer to perceive your universe. Thus, some people visualise and 'see' things in context (List 2) . Others need to 'feel' their way round a problem (List 3), while still others, those who remembered most from List 4, like to attach sounds to what they learn or remember.

All but the first list combine right-brain activity as well as left-brain activity. People can draw mental pictures, feel and sense or hear at the same time as attempting the cold process of intellectu-alisation. Fantasy is possible.

Allowing fantasy, the connection of the left and right brain, using visual, sensing and auditory communications allows us to remember more and in the context of this book – to be more cre-ative. We will discuss how we encourage fantasy later.

Review of Conceptual Blocks

So far we have suggested that certain conceptual blocks prevent individuals from solving problems creatively. These blocks, sum-marised in Table 4 (page 28), narrow the scope of problem defini-tion, limit the consideration of alternative solutions and constrain the selection of an optimal solution. Unfortunately, many of these conceptual blocks are unconscious, and it is only by being confront-ed with unsolvable problems because of conceptual blocks, that individuals become aware that they exist. We have attempted to make you aware of your own conceptual blocks by asking you to solve problems that require you to overcome these mental barriers. These conceptual blocks, of course, are not all bad; not all problems can be addressed by creative problem-solving. But research has shown that individuals who have developed creative problem-solv-ing skills are far more effective with problems that are complex and that require a search for alternative solutions, than others who are conceptually blocked (Dauw, 1976; Basadur, 1979; Guilford, 1962; Steiner, 1978).

In the next section we provide some techniques and tools that overcome these blocks and help improve creative problem-solving skills. In the last section we discuss how creativity and innovation can be fostered in others.

Conceptual Blockbusting

Conceptual blocks cannot be overcome all at once because most blocks are a product of years of habit-forming thought processes. Overcoming them requires practice in thinking in different ways over a long period of time. You will not become a skilled creative problem-solver, of course, just by reading this book. On the other hand, by becoming aware of your conceptual blocks and practising the following techniques, you can enhance your creative problem-solving skills.

Stages in Creative Thought

A first step in overcoming conceptual blocks is simply to recognise that creative problem-solving is a skill that can be developed. Being a creative problem-solver is not a quality that some people have and some don't. As Dauw (1976, p. 19) has noted,

> Research results [show] . . . that nurturing creativity is not a question of increasing one's ability to score high on an IQ test, but a matter of improving one's mental attitudes and habits and cultivating creative skills that have lain dormant since childhood.

Haefele, (1962) reviewed the literature and found agreement that creative problem-solving involves four stages: preparation, incubation, illumination and verification.

The preparation stage includes gathering data, defining the problem, generating alternatives and consciously examining all available information. The primary difference between skilful creative problem-solving and rational problem-solving is in how this first step is approached. Creative problem-solvers are more flexible and fluent in data gathering, problem definition, alternative generation and examination of options. In fact, it is in this stage that training in creative problem-solving can significantly improve effectiveness (Allen, 1974; Basadur, 1979; McKim, 1972) because the other three steps are not amenable to conscious mental work. We will therefore limit our discussion to improving functioning in this first stage.

Secondly, the incubation stage involves mostly unconscious mental activity in which the mind combines unrelated thoughts in the pursuit of a solution. Conscious effort is not involved. Illumination, the third stage, occurs when an insight is recognised and a creative solution is articulated. Verification is the final stage, which involves evaluating the creative solution relative to some standard of acceptability.

In the preparation stage, two types of techniques are available for improving creative problem-solving abilities. One type helps individuals think about and define the problem more effectively; the other helps individuals gather information and generate more alternative solutions to the problem.

One major difference between effective, creative problem-solvers and other people is that creative problem-solvers are less constrained. They allow themselves to be more flexible in the definitions they impose on problems and the number of solutions they identify. They develop a large repertoire of approaches to problem-solving. In short, they do what Karl Weick (1979, p. 261) prescribes for unblocking decision making – they generate more conceptual options. As Interaction Associates (1971, p. 15) explained:

> Flexibility in thinking is critical to good problem-solving. A problem-solver should be able to conceptually dance around the problem like a good boxer, jabbing and poking, without getting caught in one place or 'fixated'. At any given moment, a good problem-solver should be able to apply a large number of strategies [for generating alternative definitions and solutions].
>
> Moreover, a good problem-solver is a person who has developed, through his understanding of strategies and experiences in problem-solving, a sense of appropriateness of what is likely to be the most useful strategy at any particular time.

Anyone visiting a library or bookshop will find that the number of books claiming to enhance creative problem-solving is enormous. Therefore, in the next section we present just a few tools and hints that we have found to be especially effective and relatively simple for executives and students of business to apply. Whereas some of them may seem a little game-like or playful, that is precisely what they are supposed to be – they are designed to unfreeze you and make you more like the child, asking WHY? questions without fear of seeming naive.

Methods for Improving Problem Definition

Problem definition is probably the most critical step in creative problem-solving. Once a problem is defined appropriately, solutions often come easily. However, Campbell (1952), Medawar (1967) and Schumacher (1977) point out that individuals tend to define problems in terms with which they are familiar. Medawar (1967, Introduction) notes, 'Good scientists study the most important problems they think they can solve'. When a problem is faced that is strange or does not appear to have a solution (what Schumacher calls 'divergent problems'), the problem either remains undefined or is redefined in terms of something familiar. Unfortunately, new problems may not be the same as old problems, so relying on past definitions may lead to solving the wrong problem.

> Birds Eye, part of the Unilever group in the UK, was considering a new product – 'pineapple fritters' based on fruit jelly. The pineapple jelly was cut into finger shaped pieces and was to be battered ready for frying by the consumer. The initial pilot plant to make the product was developed from a redundant conveyor system that had been used to make fish fingers – a similar SHAPED product produced by the company in vast quantities but made from hard frozen fish.
>
> The modified fish finger equipment produced a sticky and ungovernable mess when used with the fruit jelly 'fingers'. Quite suddenly someone asked – 'Why do we expect fruit jelly slices to behave the same way as rigid fingers of fish?' Once asked, the answer was obvious. Once the conceptual block was broken the whole concept of making the fruit jelly product was reviewed and the final product was manufactured in a machine derived from the confectionery industry, not the technology of frozen fish.

Applying some hints for creative problem-definition can help individuals see problems in alternative ways so their definitions are not so narrowly constrained. Three such hints for improving and expanding definition are discussed below.

Make the Strange Familiar and the Familiar Strange
One well-known technique for improving creative problem-solving is called 'Synectics' (Gordon, 1961). The goal of synectics is simply to help you put something you don't know in terms of something you do know and vice versa. By analysing what you know and applying it to what you don't know, new insights and perspectives can be developed.

It works like this. First you form a definition of a problem (make the strange familiar). Then you try to make that definition out-of-focus, distorted or transposed in some way (make the familiar strange). Use analogies and metaphors to create this distortion. Then you postpone the original definition of the problem while you analyse the analogy or metaphor. You impose the analysis on the original problem to see what new insights you can uncover.

For example, suppose you have defined a problem as low morale among members of your team. You may form an analogy or metaphor by answering questions such as the following about the problem:

- What does this remind me of?
- What does this make me feel like?
- What is this similar to?
- What isn't this similar to?

Examples of the answers to these questions might be:

- This problem reminds me of trying to turn a rusty bolt. How do you turn a rusty bolt – apply lubricant. What is a 'lubricant' for my team? – a party, a weekend get-together?
- It makes me feel like I do when visiting a hospital ward. I usually feel bad when I visit a ward because I expect the worst. The ward is drab and badly signposted – so is our workplace. Are we talking of simple redecoration and perhaps photographs on who is who?
- This is similar to going back into the losing side's dressing room after a terrible defeat. Okay, we have failed once or twice, but have we celebrated victory? Have we had a good sort out on what went wrong? Were the right people disciplined? Have we learnt?

Metaphors and analogies should connect what you are less sure about (the original problem) to what you are more sure about (the metaphor). By analysing the metaphor or analogy, you may identify attributes of the problem that were not evident before. New insights often occur.

The analogies can be taken from a checklist provided by Gordon (1961) and others.

> A major clearing bank in the UK was concerned with the problem of direct mail going to customers who had already been refused the bank's credit facilities. Using the metaphor of 'goal keeping' from a list, they drew the comparison of an 'own goal'. Goal keepers and the defence have to maintain a continual dialogue to avoid 'own goals'. This dialogue was perfectly easy for the bank to envisage and the problem was solved.

The ideas of Gordon are not new. William Harvey used the pump analogy to the heart, which allowed him new insights into the body's circulation system. Niels Bohr compared the atom to the solar system and supplanted Rutherford's prevailing 'raisin pudding' model of matter's building blocks. Creativity consultant Roger von Oech (1986) helped turn around a struggling computer company by applying a restaurant analogy to the company's operations. By analysing the problems of a restaurant – 'safe' environment – the management of the computer company were able to highlight the problems of their own company by comparison. Major contributions in the field of organisational behaviour have occurred by applying analogies to other types of organisation, such as machines, cybernetic or open systems, force fields, clans and so on. Probably the most effective analogies (called parables) were used by Jesus to teach principles that otherwise were difficult for individuals to grasp, given their culture and heritage.

Some hints to keep in mind when constructing analogies are these:
1. Include action or motion in the analogy (for example, driving a car, cooking a meal, attending a funeral)
2. Include things that can be visualised or pictured in the analogy (for example, stars, football games, crowded shopping centres)
3. Pick familiar events or situations (for example, families, kissing, bedtime)
4. Try to relate things that are not obviously similar (for example, saying an organisation is like a crowd is not nearly so rich a simile as saying an organisation is like a psychic prison or a poker game).

Four types of analogies are recommended as part of Synectics:

- **Personal analogies,** where individuals try to identify themselves as the problem – 'If I were the problem, how would I feel, what would I like, what could satisfy me?'
- **Direct analogies,** where individuals apply facts, technology and common experience to the problem (e.g., Brunel solved the problem of underwater construction by watching a shipworm tunnelling into a tube)
- **Symbolic analogies,** where symbols or images are imposed on the problem (e.g., modelling the problem mathematically or diagramming the logic flow).
- **Fantasy analogies,** where individuals ask the question – ' In my wildest dreams, how would I wish the problem to be resolved?' We might say for example – ' I wish all employees would work with no supervision'.

Elaborate on the Definition

There are a variety of ways to enlarge, alter or replace a problem definition once it has been specified. One way is to force yourself to generate at least two alternative hypotheses for every problem definition. That is, specify at least two plausible definitions of the problem in addition to the one originally accepted. Think in plural terms rather than in singular terms. Instead of asking, 'What is the problem?', 'What is the meaning of this?', 'What is the result?', ask questions like, 'What are the problems?', 'What are the meanings of this?', 'What are the results?'

As an example, look at Figure 6 (next page). Which shape is the odd-one out?

A majority of people select b) first because it is the only figure that is all straight lines – they are of course correct. Others may pick a) as it is the only figure with a continuous line, no points of discontinuity; they are also correct. The choice of c), as the only figure with two straight and two curved lines; d), as the only figure with one curved and one straight line; or e), as the only figure that is non-symmetrical or partial – are ALL correct choices. The point is, there can often be more than one problem definition, more than one right answer and more than one perspective from which to view a problem.

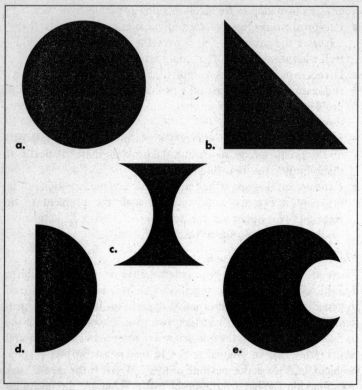

FIGURE 6 The five-figure problem

Another way to elaborate definitions is to use a question check-list. This is simply a series of questions designed to help individuals think of alternatives to their accepted definitions. Several creative managers have shared with us some of their most fruitful questions:

1. Is there anything else?
2. Is the reverse true?
3. Is there a more general problem?
4. Can it be stated differently?
5. Who sees it differently?
6. What past experience is this like?

As an exercise, take a minute now to think of a problem you are currently experiencing. Write it down so it is formally specified. Now manipulate that definition by answering each of the six questions in the checklist. If you can't think of a problem, try the exercise with this one: 'I am not as attractive as I would like to be'.

Reverse the Definition
A third tool for improving and expanding problem definition is to reverse the definition of the problem. That is, turn the problem upside down, inside out or back to front. Reverse the way in which you think of the problem. For example, consider the following fable:

> Many years ago, a small businessman found himself with a large debt to a creditor. The creditor, rumoured to have been associated with organised crime, became adamant that repayment be made by a deadline that was impossible for the businessman to meet. Business was not good and the businessman could not even keep up the interest payments, let alone the loan principal. The creditor, however, had become attracted to the businessman's daughter and in his conniving ways, decided he would rather have the girl than the small, failing business. The daughter, however, was repulsed by such a suggestion and resisted all his advances.
>
> The creditor was a gambling man and always enjoyed the thrill of a contest. He decided to propose a game to the businessman and his daughter that would decide her fate and that of the business. He indicated that he would put a white pebble and a black pebble into a bag and then have the young woman pick out a pebble. If she chose the black pebble, she would become his wife and the businessman's debt would be considered paid in full. If she chose the white pebble, she could stay with her father and the debt would be cancelled. If she refused to participate in the game, the entire balance would be made due by the end of the month.
>
> Reluctantly, the businessman agreed to the creditor's proposal. They met on the a pebble-strewn path of a local park to conduct this game of chance. As they chatted, the creditor stooped down, picked up two pebbles and put them into a bag. The young woman, sharp-eyed with fright, noticed that the creditor had put two black pebbles in the bag. He held up the bag and asked the young woman to select the pebble that would decide her fate and that of her father's business.

(Based upon deBono, 1968)

Accepting that the story is a fable from a world before 'political correctness' had been invented, what would you advise the girl to do?

A common approach is to maintain a constant definition of the problem and try to manipulate the circumstances. Most individuals suggest one of these alternatives:

1. The young woman should accuse the creditor of cheating. The negative consequence of this is that she risks antagonising the man and her father losing his business.
2. The young woman should try to change the rules of the contest. However, she should accept that the creditor is no fool and he is unlikely to make life more difficult for himself when he sees himself in a powerful position.
3. The young woman should try to cheat by picking up a white pebble from the ground. This is perfectly possible if the young woman is a practised conjuror but risky otherwise.
4. She should sacrifice herself and then try to get out of the marriage later.

All the suggestions maintain a single definition of the problem. Each assumes that the solution to the problem is associated with the pebble that the girl selects. If the problem is reversed, other answers normally not considered become evident. That is, the pebble remaining in the bag could also determine her fate.

In the fable, the girl selects a pebble from the bag, but then quickly drops it to the ground on the pebble-strewn path. She exclaims, 'Oh, how clumsy of me. But never mind, the one I chose will be obvious. All you have to do is look in the bag and see the colour of the one left.' By reversing the definition, she changed a situation with zero probability of success to a situation with 100 per cent probability of success.

This reversal is similar to what Rothenburg (1979) refers to as 'Janusian thinking'. Janus was the Roman god with two faces that looked in opposite directions. Janusian thinking means thinking contradictory thoughts at the same time – that is, conceiving two opposing ideas to be true concurrently. Rothenburg claimed, after studying 54 highly creative artists and scientists (e.g., Nobel Prize winners), that most major scientific breakthroughs and artistic masterpieces are products of Janusian thinking. Creative people who actively formulate antithetical ideas and then resolve them produce the most valuable contributions to the scientific and artistic worlds. Quantum leaps in knowledge often occur.

An example is Einstein's account (1919, p. 1) of 'having the happiest thought of my life.' He developed the concept that, for an observer in free fall from the roof of a house, there exists during his fall, no gravitational field in his immediate vicinity. If the observer releases any objects, they will remain, relative to him, in a state of rest. 'The [falling] observer is therefore justified in considering his state as one of rest.' Einstein concluded, in other words, that two seemingly contradictory states could be present simultaneously: motion and rest. This realisation lead to the development of his revolutionary general theory of relativity.

In another study, Rothenburg (1979) gave individuals a stimulus word and asked them to respond with the words that first came to mind. He found that highly creative students, Nobel scientists and prize-winning artists responded with antonyms significantly more often than did individuals with average creativity. Rothenburg argued, from these results, that creative people think in terms of opposites more often than do other people.

For our purposes, the whole point is to reverse or contradict the currently accepted definition in order to expand the number of perspectives considered. For instance, a problem might be that morale is too high instead of (or in addition to) too low in our team, or that employees need less motivation instead of more motivation to increase productivity. Opposites and backward looks often enhance creativity.

The techniques for improving creative problem definition are summarised below.
1. Make the strange familiar and the familiar strange.
2. Elaborate on the definition.
3. Reverse the definition.

Their purpose is not to help you generate alternative definitions just for the sake of alternatives, but to broaden your perspectives, to help you overcome conceptual blocks and to produce more high quality, relevant and 'simple' solutions.

Generate More Alternatives

A common tendency is to define problems in terms of available solutions (i.e., the problem is defined as a solution already possessed) or the first acceptable alternative (e.g., March & Simon, 1958). This tendency leads to consideration of a minimal number and narrow range of alternatives in problem-solving. However, Guilford (1962), a pioneer in the study of creative problem-solving, asserted that the primary characteristics of effective creative problem-solvers are their fluency and their flexibility of thought. Fluency refers to the number of ideas or concepts produced in a given length of time. Flexibility refers to the diversity of ideas or concepts generated. While most problem-solvers consider a few homogeneous alternatives, creative problem-solvers consider many heterogeneous alternatives. The following techniques are designed to help you improve your ability to generate many varied alternatives when faced with problems. They are summarised below.

1. Defer judgement.
2. Expand current alternatives.
3. Combine unrelated attributes.

Defer Judgement

Probably the most common method of generating alternatives is the technique of **brainstorming**. Developed by Osborn (1953), this is a powerful tool. Most people make quick judgements about each piece of information or each alternative solution they encounter: brainstorming is designed to help people generate alternatives for problem-solving without prematurely evaluating, and hence discarding, them. Four main rules govern brainstorming:

1. No evaluation of any kind is permitted as alternatives are being generated. Individual energy is spent on generating ideas, not on defending them.
2. The wildest possible ideas are encouraged. It is easier to tighten alternatives up than to loosen them.

3. The quantity of ideas takes precedence over the quality. Emphasising quality engenders judgement and evaluation.
4. Participants should build on or modify the ideas of others. Poor ideas that are added to or altered often become good ideas.

Brainstorming techniques are best used in a group setting so individuals can stimulate ideas from each other. Maier (1967) showed that generating alternatives in a group setting produces more and better ideas than can be produced alone. The very quantity and rate of production of ideas – 100 ideas in a 30 minute session would be normal – means that people are unable to refer their own or other peoples ideas to their own conceptual blocks. Ideas are left unscreened.

In a brainstorming session one member of the group acts as a facilitator, recording the ideas – preferably numbered and on a flipchart. Under no circumstances must the facilitator contribute to idea generation, his or her job is that of a scribe, a servant of the group who is allowed to clarify but not modify.

A brainstorming session often works in spurts of creativity. In the first stage, fairly mundane ideas appear, often ideas that are already in the minds of the individuals in the group. There is often then a surge of ideas, building on the previous batch; the surge then stops but can be revived by the facilitator asking for votes on the 'worst idea' yet. By discussing what is positive on the bad idea a new stage of creativity is often reached.

The best way to get a feel for the power of brainstorming groups is to participate in one. Spend at least 20 minutes in a small group, brainstorming ideas.

Take five minutes and list how many uses you can think of for a table-tennis ball. The greater the number of uses, the greater your fluency. The greater the variety, the greater your flexibility.

What ideas can you come up with? Generate as many ideas as you can using the rules of brainstorming and after about 20 minutes or about 100 ideas, assess the insights that the session may have produced. Examples of lists we have generated on training courses include: a bob for a fishing line, Christmas decoration, a toy for a cat, gear-lever knob, part of a molecular structure model, wind gauge when hung from a string, head of a puppet and a miniature football. Your list may well be much longer.

Sometimes brainstorming in a group is not possible or is too costly in terms of the number of people involved and the time required. Managers pursuing a hectic organisational life may feel that brainstorming is a waste of time and outside the organisational culture. This is a great pity, but even the process of individuals siting together in relaxed circumstances jotting down ideas on a flip chart is better than nothing.

Tony Buzan (1974) introduced the concept of 'mind mapping', a technique that has been developed considerably with the introduction of Total Quality Management Systems. John Oakland (1994) cites a variation of brainstorming – the use of the cause and effect analysis. The technique was developed by Sumitomo Electric and is known as CEDAC – a cause and effect diagram with the addition of cards.

The concept of the cause and effect diagram is due to Ishikawa and provides a logical and acceptable way of structuring ideas from a brainstorming session devoted to solving a problem. Suppose we have a problem concerned with quality. The causes of the quality problem are grouped on the spines of a 'fishbone' classified as procedures, equipment and plant, materials, information and people. The effect side of the diagram is a quantified description of a problem with an agreed and quantified target. The cause side of the diagram uses two different coloured cards for writing FACTS and IDEAS.

FACTS are placed on the left of the diagram and IDEAS on the right, each card being initialed by the individual owning it.

The cause and effect diagram systems have one considerable advantage over the brainstorming approaches from which they were built – they are seen to be practical and sensible. Many of the more esoteric systems, and in particular Synectics, although very effective in practice, are difficult to justify in a hard nosed environment.

Build on the Current Alternatives.
One useful technique for building on the alternatives that comes from simple brainstorming is the technique of **sub-division**. This simply means dividing a problem into smaller parts. March and

Simon (1958, p. 193) suggest that sub-division improves problem-solving by increasing the speed with which alternatives can be generated and selected. They explain that

> The mode of sub-division has an influence on the extent to which planning can proceed simultaneously on several aspects of the problem. The more detailed the factorisation of the problem, the more simultaneous activity is possible, the greater the speed of problem-solving.

To see how sub-division helps develop more alternatives and speeds the process of problem-solving, go back to your list of ideas but now sub-divide the table-tennis ball into attributes – it has weight, colour, texture, shape, porosity, strength, hardness, chemical properties and conduction potential. Think how each attribute might be incorporated into a new use.

Using this technique many more diverse uses are likely to arrive, for example:

■ Shape – a reflector holder or a pastry cutter when cut in half,
■ Colour – a marker for a helipad
■ Strength – a collision damper

One exercise we have sometimes used with students and executives to illustrate this technique is to have them write down as many of their managerial strengths as they can think of. Most people list ten or 12 attributes relatively easily. Then we analyse the various dimensions of the manager's role, the activities that managers engage in, the challenges that most managers face from inside and outside the organisation, and so on. We then ask these same people to write down another list of their strengths as managers. The list is almost always twice as long or more. The point is, by identifying the sub-components of any problem, far more alternatives can be generated than by considering the problem as a whole. You can try this exercise yourself.

Divide Figure 7 (next page) into exactly four pieces equal in size, shape and area. Try to do it in a minute or less. The problem is easy if you use subdivision. It is more difficult if you don't. For one possible answer see the Scoring Key at the end of the book (page 96).

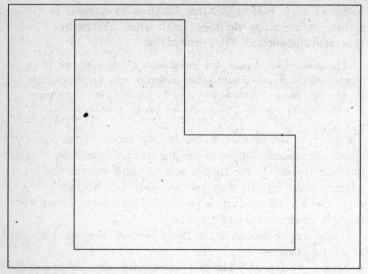

FIGURE 7   Fractionation problem

Combine Unrelated Attributes

A third technique focuses on helping problem-solvers expand alternatives by forcing the integration of seemingly unrelated elements. Research into creative problem-solving has shown that an ability to see common relationships among disparate factors is a major factor differentiating creative individuals from the non-creative (see Dellas & Gaier, 1970, for a review of this research). This can be done using a **relational algorithm** (Crovitz, 1970).

The relational algorithm involves applying connecting words that force a relationship between two elements in a problem. For example, the following is a list of some relational words:

about	among	because	by	if	now
across	and	before	down	in	of
after	as	between	for	near	off
against	at	but	from	not	on
opposite	over	so	through	under	where
or	round	then	till	up	while
out	still	though	to	when	with

To illustrate the use of this technique, suppose you are faced with the following problem: 'Our customers are dissatisfied with our service'. The two major elements in this problem are *customers* and *service*. They are connected by the phrase 'are dissatisfied with'. With the relational algorithm technique, the relational words in the problem statement are removed and replaced with other relational words to see if new ideas for alternative solutions can be identified.

For example, consider the following connections where new relational words are used:

- Customers among service (e.g., customers interact with service personnel)
- Customers as service (e.g., customers deliver service to other customers)
- Customers and service (e.g., customers and service personnel work together)
- Customers for service (e.g., customer focus groups help improve our service)
- Service near customers (e.g., change the location of the service)
- Service before customers (e.g., prepare service before the customer arrives)
- Service through customers (e.g., use customers to provide additional service)
- Service when customers (e.g., provide timely service)

By connecting the two elements of the problem in different ways, new possibilities for problem-solution can be formulated.

Hints for Applying Problem-Solving Techniques

In theory, Thamia and Woods (1984) found that a very large number of techniques 'appeared' to have been used during the three years of their study in one major organisation. In practice the truth was quite different:

- There was a perceived need for creativity and the pressure for novel solutions came from the top management.

- Rational and creative problem-solving were seen as activities in their own right with procedures for booking time spent in sessions employing the techniques.
- A core group of two people was set up to provide 'hand holding support' for groups and individuals requiring help in solving problems
- Very rarely was a 'pure' technique applied – only the key process of analysis, synthesis, collation and judgement was maintained and disciplines of brainstorming were imposed throughout.

Our intention in presenting several of the key techniques is to help you expand the number of options available to you for defining problems and for generating additional potential solutions. They are most useful when problems arise that require a new approach or a new perspective. All of us have enormous creative potential, but the stresses and pressures of daily life, coupled with the inertia of conceptual habits, tend to submerge that potential. These hints are merely ways to help unlock it again.

Reading about techniques or wanting to be creative won't improve your creativity, of course. These techniques and tools are not magic in themselves. They depend on your ability to actually generate new ideas and to think different thoughts. Because that is so difficult for most of us, here are six practical hints to help prepare you to create more conceptual flexibility and to better apply these techniques.

1. Give yourself some relaxation time. The more intense your work, the more your need for complete breaks. Break out of your routine sometimes. This frees up your mind and gives room for new thoughts.
2. Find a place (physical space) where you can think. It should be a place where interruptions are eliminated, at least for a time. Reserve your best time for thinking.
3. Talk to other people about ideas. Isolation produces far fewer ideas than does conversation. Make a list of people who stimulate you to think. Spend some time with them.
4. Ask other people for their ideas about your problems. Find out

what others think about them. Don't be embarrassed to share your problems, but don't become dependent on others to solve them for you.
5. Read a lot. Read at least one thing regularly that is outside your field of expertise. Keep track of new thoughts from your reading.
6. Protect yourself from idea-killers. Don't spend time with 'black holes' – people who absorb all of your energy and light but give nothing in return. Don't let yourself or others negatively evaluate your ideas too soon.

You'll find these hints useful not only for enhancing creative problem-solving, but for rational problem-solving as well. Figure 8 (next page) summarises the two problem-solving processes – rational and creative – and the factors you should consider when determining how to approach each type of problem.

In brief, when you encounter a problem that is straightforward – that is, outcomes are predictable, sufficient information is available, and means-ends connections are clear – rational problem-solving techniques are most appropriate. You should apply the four distinct, sequential steps. On the other hand, when the problem is not straightforward – that is, information is ambiguous and/or unavailable, and alternative solutions are not apparent – you should apply creative problem-solving techniques in order to improve problem definition and alternative generation.

Fostering Innovation

Unlocking your own creative potential is not enough, of course, to make you a successful manager. A major challenge is to help unlock it in other people as well. Fostering innovation and creativity among those with whom you work is at least as great a challenge as increasing your own creativity. In this last section of the book we will discuss some principles that will help you bring innovation out of others and encourage it to flourish in the organisation.

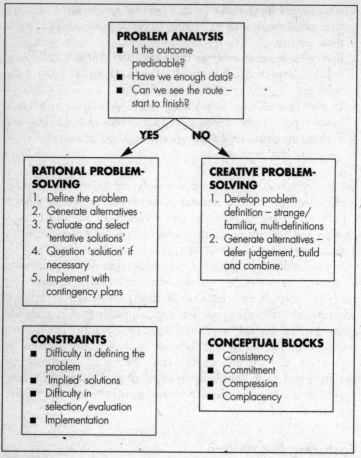

FIGURE 8   A summary of the rational and creative problem-solving processes

Management Principles for Innovation

Neither Percy Spencer nor Spence Silver could have succeeded in their creative ideas had there not been a managerial support system present that fostered creative problem-solving and the pursuit of innovation. In each case, certain characteristics were present in their organisations, fostered by managers around them, that made their innovations possible. In this section we will not discuss the macro-organisational issues associated with innovation e.g., organisation design, strategic orientation and human resource systems. Excellent discussions of those factors are reviewed in sources such as Galbraith (1982), Kanter (1983), McMillan (1985), Tichy (1983), and Amabile (1988). Instead, we'll focus on some of the activities in which individual managers can engage that foster innovativeness. Table 6 summarises three management principles that can help engender more innovativeness and creative problem-solving.

Table 6 Three principles for fostering innovativeness

Principle	Examples
1. Pull people apart; put people together.	■ Let individuals work alone as well as with teams and task forces.
	■ Encourage minority reports and legitimise devil's advocate roles.
	■ Encourage heterogeneous membership in teams.
	■ Separate competing groups or subgroups.
2. Monitor and prod.	■ Talk to customers.
	■ Identify customer expectations both in advance and after the sale.
	■ Hold people accountable.
	■ Use 'sharp-pointed' prods.
3. Reward multiple roles.	■ Idea champion.
	■ Sponsor and mentor.
	■ Orchestrator and facilitator.
	■ Rule breaker

Pull People Apart – Put People Together

Percy Spencer's magnetron project was a consumer product hidden away from Raytheon's main-line business of missiles and other defence contract work. Spence Silver's new glue resulted when a polymer adhesive task force was separated from 3M's normal activities. The Macintosh computer was developed by a task force that was taken outside the company and given space and time to work on an innovative computer. Many new ideas come from individuals being given some time and resources and allowed to work apart from the normal activities of the organisation. 3M gives its staff 'skunk time' – periods which are not formally accounted for and should be reserved for 'wild ideas' and 'personal projects' which just might work. Establishing nursery slopes, practice fields or sandlots is as good a way to develop new skills in business as it has proved to be in athletics. Because most businesses are designed to produce the 10,000th part correctly or to service the 10,000th customer efficiently, they do not function very well at producing the first part. That is why pulling people apart is often necessary to foster innovation and creativity. Data General divided their development effort for the new Eagle mini computers into two competing groups on two separate sites.

On the other hand, forming teams (putting people together) is almost always more productive than people working by themselves. But the teams should be characterised by certain attributes. For example, Nemeth (1986) found that creativity increased markedly when minority influences were present in the team, for example, when devil's advocate roles were legitimised, a formal minority report was always included in final recommendations, and individuals assigned to work on a team had divergent backgrounds or views.

> 'Those exposed to minority views are stimulated to attend to more aspects of the situation, they think in more divergent ways and they are more likely to detect novel solutions or to come to new decisions' (Nemeth, 1986, p. 25).

Nemeth found that those positive benefits occur in groups even when the divergent or minority views are wrong. Similarly, Janis (1971) found that narrow-mindedness in groups (called groupthink) was best overcome by establishing competing groups working on the same problem, participation in groups by outsiders, assigning a role of critical evaluator in the group, having groups made up of cross-functional participants, and so on. The most productive groups are those that are characterised by fluid roles, lots of interaction among members and flat power structures.

The point is, innovativeness can be fostered when individuals are placed in teams and when they are at least temporarily separated from the normal pressures of organisational life. Those teams, however, are most effective at generating innovative ideas when they are characterised by attributes of minority influence, competition, heterogeneity and interaction. You can help foster innovation among people you manage, therefore, by letting people have their own space as well as putting people together in temporary teams.

Monitor and Prod

Neither Percy Spencer nor Spence Silver were allowed to work on their projects with no accountability. Both men eventually had to report on the results they accomplished with their experimentation and imagination. At 3M people are expected to spend 15 per cent of their time as 'skunk time' away from company business to work on new, creative ideas. In this time they can, with some limits, appropriate company materials and resources to work on them. However, individuals are held accountable for their lawlessness and need to show results.

Holding people accountable for outcomes, in fact, is an important motivator for improved performance. Data General made it clear to their two project leaders for the Eagle project that their jobs were on the line. Two innovators in the entertainment industry captured this principle with these remarks: 'The ultimate inspiration is the deadline. That's when you have to do what needs to be done. The fact that twice a year the creative talent of this country is working until midnight to get something ready for a trade show is very good for the economy. Without this kind of pressure, things would turn to mashed potatoes' (von Oech, 1986, p. 119).

In addition to accountability, innovativeness is stimulated by what Gene Goodson at Johnson Controls called 'sharp-pointed prods'. After taking over the automotive group at that company, Goodson found that he could stimulate creative problem-solving by issuing certain mandates that demanded innovativeness. One such mandate was: 'There will be no more forklift trucks allowed in any of our plants'. At first hearing, that mandate sounds absolutely outrageous. Think about it. You have a plant with tens of thousands of square feet of floor space. The loading docks are on one side of the building, and many tons of heavy metal raw materials are unloaded weekly and moved from the loading docks to workstations throughout the entire factory. The only way it can be done is with forklifts. Eliminating forklift trucks would ruin the plant, right? Wrong. This sharp-pointed prod simply demanded that individuals working in the plant find ways to move the work stations closer to the raw materials, to move the unloading of the raw materials closer to the workstations or to change the size and amounts of material being unloaded. The innovations that resulted from eliminating forklifts saved the company millions of dollars in materials handling and wasted time, dramatically improved quality, productivity and efficiency, and made it possible for Johnson Controls to capture business from their Japanese competitors.

One of the best methods for generating useful prods is to regularly monitor customer preferences, expectations and evaluations. Many of the most creative ideas have come from customers, the recipients of goods and services. Identifying their preferences in advance and monitoring their evaluations of products or services later are both good ways to get ideas for innovation and to be prodded to make improvements. All employees should be in regular contact with their own customers, asking questions and monitoring performance.

By customers, we don't mean just the end-users of a business product or service. In fact, all of us have customers, whether we are students in college, members of a family, players on a rugby team, or whatever. Customers are simply those for whom we are trying to produce something or whom we serve. Students, for example, can count on their tutors, their fellow class mates and their potential employers as customers whom they serve. A *priori* and *post hoc* monitoring of their expectations and evaluations is an important way to help foster new ideas for problem-solving. This monitoring is best done by personal contact, but it can also be done by follow-up calls, surveys, customer complaint cards and suggestion systems, or whatever fits the organisational culture and the issue.

The basic point is simply that you can foster innovativeness by holding people accountable for new ideas and by stimulating them with periodic prods. The most useful prods generally come from customers.

Reward Multiple Roles

The success of the sticky yellow notes at 3M is more than a story of the creativity of Spence Silver. In fact, without a number of people playing multiple roles, the glue would probably still be on a shelf somewhere. Instead, it provides a good illustration of the necessity of multiple roles in innovation and the importance of recognising and rewarding them. The four crucial roles in the innovative process are the idea champion (the person who comes up with the innovative problem solution); the sponsor or mentor (the person who helps provide the resources, environment, and encouragement for the idea champion to work on the idea); the orchestrator or facilitator (the person who brings together cross-functional groups and necessary political support to facilitate implementation of the creative idea); and the rule breaker (the person who goes beyond organisational boundaries and barriers to ensure success of the innovation). Each of these roles is present in most important innovations in organisations, and they are illustrated by the Post-It Note example below.

1. Spence Silver, by experimenting with chemical configurations that the academic literature indicated wouldn't work, invented a glue that wouldn't stick. He stuck with it, however, and spent years giving presentations to any audience at 3M that would listen, trying to pawn it off on some division that could find a practical application for it. The trouble was, no one else got stuck on it.

2. Henry Courtney and Roger Merrill developed a coating substance that allowed the glue to stick to one surface but not to others. This made it possible to produce a permanently temporary glue – that is, one that would peel off easily when pulled but would otherwise hang on forever.

3. Art Fry found the problem that fit Spence Silver's solution. He found application for the glue as a better 'bookmark' and as a note pad. The trouble was, no equipment existed at 3M to coat

only a part of a piece of paper with the glue. Fry, therefore, carried 3M equipment and tools home to his own basement, where he designed and made his own machine to manufacture the forerunner of Post-It Notes. Because the working machine became too large to get out of his basement, he blasted a hole in the wall to get the equipment back to 3M. He then brought together engineers, designers, production managers and machinists to demonstrate the prototype machine and generate enthusiasm to make the product.

4. Geoffrey Nicholson and Joseph Ramsey began marketing the product inside 3M. They also submitted the product to the standard 3M market tests. The trouble was, the product failed miserably. No one wanted to pay $1. 00 for a notepad. However, they broke 3M rules by personally visiting test market sites and giving away free samples. Only then did the consuming public become addicted to the product.

This brief scenario illustrates the importance of these four roles in the innovation process. Spence Silver was both a rule breaker and an idea champion. Art Fry was also an idea champion, but more importantly he orchestrated the coming-together of the various groups needed to get the innovation off the ground. Henry Courtney and Roger Merrill helped sponsor Silver's innovation by providing him with the coating substance that would allow his idea to work. Geoff Nicholson and Joe Ramsey were both rule breakers and sponsors in their bid to get the product accepted by the public. In each case, not only did all these people play unique roles, but they did so with tremendous enthusiasm and zeal. They were both confident of their ideas and willing to put their time and resources on the line as advocates. They fostered support among a variety of constituencies both within their own areas of expertise as well as among outside groups. Most organisations are inclined to give in to those who are sure of themselves, persistent in their efforts and persuasiveness enough to make converts of others.

Not everyone can be an idea champion. But when managers also reward and recognise those who sponsor and orchestrate the ideas of others, innovativeness increases in organisations. Teams form, supporters replace competitors and creativity thrives. Facilitating multiple role development is the job of the innovative manager. The converse is also true as the following example shows:

> A major multi-national working from the UK was looking to diversify and one idea that came forwards was to use the Dolby sound system for a new generation of hearing aids. The idea although exciting had several 'issues' that needed to be settled before its adoption.
>
> The senior manager in charge of the project asked who would like to run with the idea and to head a venture company to sell it. Nobody wanted to stake their reputation on the idea so it was quietly killed in spite of the apparent general enthusiasm of the team.

Summary

It is no accident that many of techniques and studies described in this book date from the late 1970s and early 1980s. This was the period when the West began to stocktake and realise that it no longer had a monopoly of invention. The situation was highlighted in the UK by the Finneston Report (1980). Monty Finneston produced a well-argued case that not only had the UK declined as 'the workshop of the world', but that unless major effort was redirected into the engineering wealth-creation industries, the decline would accelerate. A key statistic was that whereas in the late 1970s UK, Sweden, France and the USA had between 1.3 per cent (France) and 1.7 per cent (UK) of the population as graduate engineers, Japan had 4.2 per cent (Germany was at 2.3 per cent.)

Engineering graduate numbers are obviously not the whole story, but the Finneston Report and the climate that commissioned it stirred activity in the West that has not faded. Innovation, and not just innovation in engineering, is the key to the survival of our economies. Innovation and problem-solving, as treated in this book, are key stones to innovation.

We have shown that a well developed model exists for solving problems. It consists of four separate and sequential stages: defining the problem; generating alternative solutions; evaluating and selecting a solution; implementing it and following it up. This model, however, is mainly useful for solving straightforward problems. Many problems faced by managers are not of this type and frequently they are called on to exercise creative problem-solving skills. That is, they must broaden their perspective of the problem and develop alternative solutions that are not immediately obvious.

We have discussed and illustrated eight major conceptual blocks that inhibit most people's creative problem-solving abilities. Conceptual blocks are mental obstacles that artificially constrain problem definition and solution, and keep most people from being effective creative problem-solvers. The four major conceptual blocks were summarised in Table 4 (page 28).

Overcoming these conceptual blocks is a matter of skill development and practice in thinking, not a matter of innate ability. Everyone can become a skilled creative problem-solver with practice. Becoming aware of these thinking inhibitors helps individuals overcome them. We also discussed three major principles for improving creative problem-definition and three major principles for improving the creative generation of alternative solutions. Certain techniques were described that can help implement these six principles.

We concluded by offering some hints about how to foster creativity and innovativeness among other people. Becoming an effective problem-solver yourself is important, but effective managers can also enhance this activity among their subordinates, peers and superiors.

Behavioural Guidelines

1. Follow the four-step procedure outlined in Table 2 (pages 11–12) when solving straightforward problems. Keep the steps separate and do not take shortcuts.
2. When approaching a difficult problem, try to overcome your conceptual blocks by consciously doing the following mental activities:
   - Use lateral thinking in addition to vertical thinking.
   - Use several thought languages instead of just one.
   - Challenge stereotypes based on past experiences.
   - Identify underlying themes and commonalities in seemingly unrelated factors.
   - Ignore the superfluous and collect missing information when studying the problem.
   - Avoid artificially constraining problem boundaries.
   - Ignore reticence to be inquisitive.
   - Use both right- and left-brain thinking.

3. When defining a problem, make the strange familiar and the

familiar strange by using metaphor and analogy, first to focus and then to distort and refocus the definition.

4. Elaborate the problem definitions by developing at least two alternative (opposite) definitions and by applying a checklist.
5. Reverse the problem definition by beginning with the end result and working backwards.
6. In generating potential problem-solutions, defer judging any until many have been proposed. Use the four rules of brainstorming:
   - Do not evaluate.
   - Encourage wild ideas.
   - Encourage quantity.
   - Build on other peoples' ideas.

7. Expand the list of current alternative solutions by subdividing the problem into its attributes.
8. Increase the number of possible solutions by combining unrelated problem attributes.
9. Foster innovativeness among those with whom you work by doing the following:
   - Find a 'practice field' where individuals can experiment and try out ideas, and assign them responsibility for fostering innovation.
   - Put people holding different perspectives in teams to work on problems.
   - Hold people accountable for innovation.
   - Use sharp-pointed prods to stimulate new thinking.
   - Recognise, reward, and encourage the participation of multiple players, including idea champion, sponsor, orchestrator and rule breaker.

Skill Analysis

Case Involving Creative Problem-Solving

The Sony Walkman

They had been disappointed at first, but it wasn't something that was going to keep them awake at nights. Mitsuro Ida and a group of electronics engineers in Sony Corporation's Tape Recorder Division in Tokyo had tried to redesign a small, portable tape recorder, called 'Pressman', so that it gave out stereophonic sounds. A year earlier, Ida and his group had been responsible for inventing the first Pressman, a wonderfully compact machine – ideal for use by journalists – which had sold very well.

But the sound in that tape machine was monaural. The next challenge for Sony's tape recorder engineers was to make a portable machine just as small, but with stereophonic sound. The very first stereo Pressman they made, in the last few months of 1978, didn't succeed. When Ida and his colleagues got the stereo circuits into the Pressman chassis (5.25 inches by 3.46 inches, and only 1.14 inches deep), they didn't have any space left to fit in the recording mechanism. They had made a stereophonic tape recorder that couldn't record anything. Ida regarded this as a good first try but a useless product. But he didn't throw it away. The stereo Pressman was a nice little machine. So the engineers found a few favourite music cassettes and played them while they worked.

After Ida and his fellow designers had turned their non-recording tape recorder into background music, they didn't entirely ignore it. They had frequent discussions about how to fit the stereo function and the recording mechanism into that overly small space. It was not an easy problem to solve, and because of that it was all the more fascinating and attractive to Ida and his group of inveterate problem-solvers. Their focus on the problem of the stereo Pressman blinded them to the solution that was already in their hands, accepting that it was a solution to a different problem.

'And then one day,' said Takichi Tezuka, manager of product planning for the Tape Recorder Division, 'into our room came Mr. Ibuka, our honorary chairman. He just popped into the room, saw us listening to this and thought it was very interesting.'

It is the province of honorary chairman everywhere, because their status is almost invariably ceremonial, to potter about the plant looking in on this group and that group, nodding over the latest incomprehensible gadget. To this mundane task, Masaru Ibuka brought an undiminished intelligence and an active imagination. When he entered the Tape Recorder Division and saw Ida's incomplete tape recorder, he admired the quality of its stereophonic sound. He also remembered an entirely unrelated project going on elsewhere in the building, where an engineer named Yoshiyuki Kamon was working to develop lightweight portable headphones.

'What if you combined them?' asked Ibuka. 'At the very least,' he said, 'the headphones would use battery power much more efficiently than stereo speakers. Reduce power requirements and you can reduce battery consumption.' But another idea began to form in his mind. If you added the headphones, wouldn't you dramatically increase the quality of what the listener hears? Could you leave out the recorder entirely and make a successful product that just plays music?

In the world of tape recorders, Ibuka's thought was heresy. He was mixing up functions. Headphones traditionally were supposed to extend the usefulness of tape recorders, not be essential to their success. This idea was so well established that if Ibuka had not made an association between a defective tape recorder design and the unfinished headphone design, Walkman may well have remained a little byway in musical history. Design groups within Sony tend to be very close-knit and remain focused on short-term task completion. Even when they weren't busy, there was no reason for tape recorder people ever to communicate with headphone people. They had nothing to do with each other. Tezuka, the man who later was described as the secretariat of the Walkman project, said, 'No one dreamed that a headphone would ever come in a package with a tape recorder. We're not very interested in what they do in the Headphone Division.'

But, even without this insularity, there was no guarantee that someone else at Sony would have made the connection that Ibuka made. To people today, the relationship between a cassette player and a set of headphones is self-evident. But to people at Sony, and at virtually every consumer electronics company, that connection was invisible in 1978.

Ibuka got a predictable response from the researchers in the electronics lab and from others in the Tape Recorder and Headphone divisions. They were painfully polite but noncommittal. Ibuka might be right that the headphones would improve Pressman's efficiency, but nobody could guess how much of an improvement that would be. No one wanted to tell Ibuka that the idea of removing the speaker in favour of headphones was crazy. But it was! What if the owner of the device wanted to play back a tape so that more than one person could listen?

When Ibuka ventured further into illogic by suggesting a playback machine with no speaker and no recorder, he lost everybody. Who would want to buy such a thing? Who in Sony Corporation would support even ten minutes of development on such a harebrained scheme?

In a way, they were right and Ibuka was wrong. This was an idea that violated most industries' well-established criteria for judging the natural increments of product development. It makes sense that a new product prototype should be better than the previous generation of product. Ida's non-recording prototype seemed worse. The idea had no support from the people who eventually would be responsible for funding its development, carrying out the research and trying to sell it to a consumer market. The idea should have been killed.

For Honorary Chairman Ibuka, the handwriting was on the wall. Even though he was a revered man at Sony, he had no authority to order such a project undertaken against the wishes of the division's leaders. It was clear that the only way to sell a bad idea to a group of cautious, reasonable businessmen was to find an ally. So, in his enthusiasm, he went straight to the office of his partner and friend, Akio Morita.

(Source: P. Ranganath Nayak and John M. Ketteringham. Breakthroughs. New York: Rawson, 1986)

Discussion Questions

1. What principles of rational problem-solving and creative problem-solving were used in this case?
2. How was innovativeness fostered within Sony by top managers?
3. What roles were played by the various characters in the case that led to the success of the Walkman?
4. If you were a consultant to Sony, what would you advise to help foster this kind of innovation more frequently and more broadly throughout the company?

Skill Practice

Exercise for Applying Conceptual Blockbusting

Background

Creative problem-solving is most applicable to problems that have no obvious solutions. Most problems people face can be solved relatively easily with a systematic analysis of alternatives. But other problems are ambiguous enough that obvious alternatives are not workable, and they require non-traditional approaches to find reasonable alternatives. This following assignment is one such problem. It is real, not fictitious, and it probably characterises your own college, university or public library. Apply the principles of creative problem-solving in the book to come up with some realistic, cost-effective and creative solutions to this problem. Don't stop at the first solutions that come to mind, because there are no obvious right answers.

Assignment

Small groups should be formed to engage in the following problem-solving exercise. Each group should generate solutions to the case. The case is factual, not fictitious. Try to be as creative in your solutions as possible. The creativity of those solutions should be judged by an independent observer, and the best group's solution should be given recognition.

In defining and solving the problems, use the following five steps. Do not skip steps.

1. Generate a single statement that accurately defines the problem. Make sure that all group members agree with the definition of the problem.
2. Only after the problem statement has been written should you propose some alternative solutions to the problem. Write these down and be prepared to report them to the larger group.
3. All small groups should report their top three alternatives

to the large group. The top three are the ones that most group members agree would produce the best solution to the problem.

4. Now, in the small group, generate at least five plausible alternative definitions of the problem. Use any of the techniques for expanding problem definition discussed in the text. Each problem statement should differ from the others in its definition, not just in its attributions or causes, of the problem.

5. After the group has agreed on the wording of the five different statements, identify at least ten new alternatives for solving the problems you have defined in step 4.

As a result of steps 4 and 5, your group should have identified some new alternatives, as well as more alternatives than you did in steps 1 and 2. Report to the large group the three alternatives that your small group judges to be the most creative.

An observer should provide feedback on the extent to which each group member applied these principles effectively, using the Observer's Feedback Form found in the Scoring Key at the end of this book (page 97).

The Bleak Future of Knowledge

Libraries throughout the world are charged with the responsibility of preserving the accumulated wisdom of the past and gathering information in the present. They serve as sources of information and resources, alternate schools, and places of exploration and discovery. No one would question the value of libraries to societies and cultures throughout the world. The materials housed there are the very foundation of civilisation. But consider the following problems.

Hundreds of thousands of books are in states of decay so advanced that when they are touched they fall to powder. Whereas parchments seem to survive better when they are handled, and books printed before 1830 on rag paper stay flexible and tough, books printed since the mid-nineteenth century on wood-pulp paper are being steadily eaten away by natural acids. British

Library, has a backlog of 1. 6 million urgent cases requiring treatment. At the newly constructed (but not yet opened) Bibliotheque Nationale in France, more than 600,000 books require treatment immediately. At the Library of Congress in the States, about 77,000 books out of the stock of 13 million enter the endangered category every year. Fairly soon, about 40 per cent of the books in the biggest research collections in America will be too fragile to handle.

An example of the scale of the problem comes from the Library of Congress which estimates that it will take 25 years to work through the backlog of cases, even if the cost of $200 a volume can be met. The obvious solution of converting to CD ROM or microfiche is not only more costly but subject to its own form of 'decay' – no 'permanent' form is yet available.

Budgets are tight throughout the world and it is doubtful that book preservation will receive high funding priority in the near future.

(Source: *The Economist*, December 23, 1989)

Skill Application

Application Activities for Solving Problems Creatively

Suggested Further Assignments

1. Teach someone else to solve problems creatively and record your experiences in your diary.
2. Think of a problem that is important to you now and has no obvious solution. Use the principles and techniques discussed in the book and work out a satisfactory creative solution. Take your time and do not expect immediate results. Record any results in your diary.
3. Help direct a group (your family, classmates, sports team) in a creative problem-solving exercise using the relevant techniques of the book. Issues could include arranging a social, raising funds, increasing membership or fixing a programme of activities. Record how it went in your diary.
4. Write a letter to a person in authority – M.P., Managing Director, Senior Police Officer – about some difficult problem in his or her authority. Make the issue something about which you have both knowledge and concern and include within your letter possible solutions. Record how you arrived at these possible solutions, as well as the solutions themselves.

Application Plan and Evaluation

The intent of this exercise is to help you apply your newly-learned skills in a real life setting. There are two parts in the activity – Part 1 will help the preparation, and Part 2 will help you evaluate and improve on the experience. Do not miss out the steps and be sure to complete each item.

Part 1 – Planning
1. Write down the two of three aspects of a skill that is most important to you. This may be an area of weakness, an area you most want

to improve or an area that is most salient to a problem that you face now. Identify the specific aspects of this skill that you want to apply.
2. Now identify the setting or the situation in which you wish to apply this skill. Establish a plan for the performance by actually writing down the situation. Who else is involved? When will you do it? Where will it be done?
3. Identify the specific behaviours you will engage in to apply the skill. Put these behaviours into detailed actions.
4. How will you judge success?

Part 2 – Evaluation
5. After you have completed your implementation, record the results. What happened? How successful were you? What was the effect on others?
6. How can you improve on your performance? What modifications would you make for next time?
7. Looking back on your experience, what have you learnt? What has been surprising? In what ways might the experience help you in the long term?

Scoring Key

Creative Problem-Solving

Skill area	Items	Assessment pre-	post-
Rational problem-solving	1, 2, 3, 4, 5	——	——
Creative problem-solving	6, 7, 8, 9, 10, 11, 12, 13, 14, 15	——	——
Fostering innovation	16, 17, 18, 19, 20, 21, 22	——	——
TOTAL SCORE		——	——

To assess how well you scored on this instrument, compare your scores to three comparison standards:

■ Compare your scores against the maximum possible (132).
■ Compare your scores with the scores of other students in your class.
■ Compare your scores to a norm group consisting of 500 business school students. In comparison to the norm group, if you scored:

   105 or above, you are in the top quartile;
   94 to 104, you are in the second quartile;
   83 to 93, you are in the third quartile;
   82 or below, you are in the bottom quartile.

How Creative Are You?

To compute your score, circle and add up the values assigned to each item. The values are as follows:

	A Agree	B Undecided or don't know	C Disagree
1.	0	1	2
2.	0	1	2
3.	4	1	0
4.	−2	0	3
5.	2	1	0
6.	−1	0	3
7.	3	0	−1
8.	0	1	2
9.	3	0	−1
10.	1	0	3
11.	4	1	0
12.	3	0	−1
13.	2	1	0
14.	4	0	−2
15.	−1	0	2
16.	2	1	0
17.	0	1	2
18.	3	0	−1
19.	0	1	2
20.	0	1	2
21.	0	1	2
22.	3	0	−1
23.	0	1	2
24.	−1	0	2
25.	0	1	3
26.	−1	0	2
27.	2	1	0
28.	2	0	−1
29.	0	1	2
30.	−2	0	3
31.	0	1	2
32.	0	1	2
33.	3	0	−1
34.	−1	0	2
35.	0	1	2

36.	1	2	3
37.	2	1	0
38.	0	1	2
39.	−1	0	2
40. See below for rating			

The following words have a value of 2:

energetic	dynamic	perceptive	dedicated
resourceful	flexible	innovative	courageous
original	observant	self-demanding	curious
enthusiastic	independent	persevering	involved

The following words have a value of 1:

self-confident	determined	informal	forward-looking
thorough	restless	alert	open-minded

The rest have values of 0.

Total Scores:

95–116	Exceptionally creative
65–94	Very creative
40–64	Above average
20–39	Average
10–19	Below average
Below 10	Noncreative

Innovative Attitude Scale

To determine your score for the Innovative Attitude Scale, add up the numbers associated with your responses to the 20 items. Then compare that score to the following norm group (consisting of graduate and undergraduate business school students, all of whom were employed full time).

Score	Percentile*
39	5
53	16
62	33
71	50
80	68
89	86
97	95

*Percentile indicates the percentage of the people who are expected to score below you.

Answers and Solutions to Problems

Solution to the Roman numeral problem (page 34)

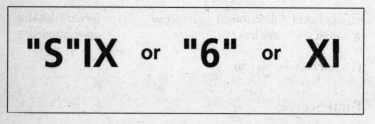

Solution to the matchstick problem in Figure 1 (page 34)

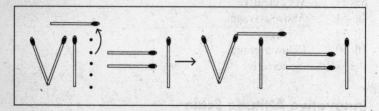

Answer to the Shakespeare problem in Figure 2 (page 38)
Five inches. (Be careful to note where page 1 of Volume I is and where the last page of Volume IV is.)

Common terms applying to both water and finance (page 39)

banks	deposits	capital drain
currency	frozen assets	sinking fund

cash flow	float a loan	liquid assets
washed up	underwater pricing	slush fund

Answer to the Descartes story (page 39)
At the foundation of Descartes' philosophy was the statement: I think, therefore I am.

Solution to the block of wood problem in Figure 3 (page 39)

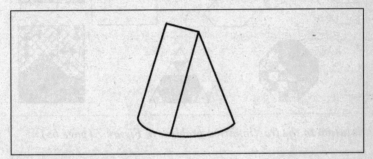

(Source: McKim, 1972)

Solutions to the nine-dot problem in Figure 4a (page 40)

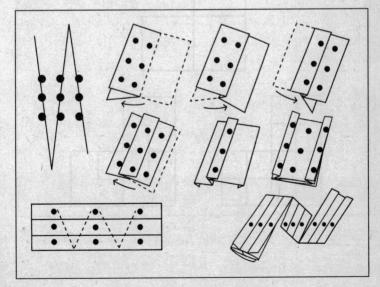

Solutions to embedded-patterns problem in Figure 5 (page 44)

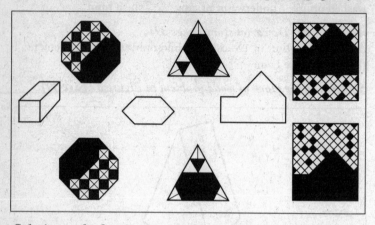

Solution to the fractionation problem in Figure 7 (page 65)

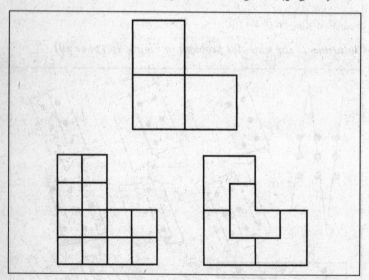

Applying Conceptual Blockbusting

The Bleak Future of Knowledge

After the group has completed its problem-solving task, take the time to give the group feedback on its performance. Also provide feedback to each individual group member, either by means of written notes or verbal comments.

Observer's Feedback Form

1. Was the problem defined explicitly?
   a. To what extent was information sought from all group members?
   b. Did the group avoid defining the problem as a disguised solution?
   c. What techniques were used to expand or alter the definitions of the problem?
2. Were alternatives proposed before any solution was evaluated?
   a. Did all group members help generate alternative solutions without judging them one at a time?
   b. Did people build on the alternatives proposed by others?
   c. What techniques were used to generate more creative alternatives for solving the problem?
3. Was the optimal solution selected?
   a. Were alternatives evaluated systematically?
   b. Was consideration given to the realistic long-term effects of each alternative?
4. Was consideration given to how and when the solution could be implemented?
   a. Were obstacles to implementation discussed?
   b. Was the solution accepted because it solved the problem under consideration, or for some other reason?
5. How creative was the group in defining the problem?
6. What techniques of conceptual blockbusting did the group use?

Glossary

Artificial constraints   Arbitrary boundaries placed around a problem that restrict possible alternative approaches and make the problem difficult to solve creatively.

Bias against thinking   The inclination to avoid mental work, one indication of the conceptual block.

Brainstorming   A technique designed to help problem solving by allowing individuals or groups to produce volumes of ideas without fear of criticism or premature evaluation.

Commitment   The conceptual block that results when an individual commits him or herself to a particular view, definition or solution.

Complacency   The conceptual block that occurs not because of poor thinking habits or inappropriate assumptions but because of fear, ignorance, self satisfaction or mental laziness.

Compression   The conceptual block that results from an individual looking at a problem too narrowly, screening out too much relevant data or making assumptions that inhibit the solving of the problem.

Conceptual blocks   Mental obstacles that restrict the way a problem is defined and limit the number of alternative solutions that might otherwise be considered.

Constancy   The conceptual block that results from using a single approach to a problem.

Contingency planning   The final stage of Potential Problem Analysis and of the implementation process. Normally the implementation of contingency plans are NOT the responsibility of the application team or indeed the appointed problem owner, but should be referred to higher authority.

Descriptive communication   Objective description of the event of behaviour that needs modification: description of the reaction to the behaviour or its consequences and a possible suggestion of alternatives.

Direct analogies   A synectic problem-solving technique in which individuals are encouraged to apply facts, technology or previous experiences to a related (or indeed unrelated) problem.

Fantasy analogies   A synectic problem-solving technique in which individuals ask: 'In my wildest dreams, how would I wish the problem to be resolved?'

Flexibility of thought   The diversity of ideas or concepts generated.

Fluency of thought	The number of ideas or concepts produced in a set period.
Group shift	The polarising effect that occurs during intensive group discussion when individuals tend to adopt a more extreme version of the position they held at the beginning of the meeting. The tendency is usually towards a risk-taking rather than a conservative stance.
Groupthink	A problem with groups. At particular times the pressure to reach consensus overrides individual critical faculties. Individuals may 'railroad' opinions and the effort to disagree with the 'groupthink' consensus is very difficult.
Homogeneity–heterogeneity	Groups composed of members with dissimilar backgrounds, skills, background – heterogeneous groups – are inclined to be better at solving complex or novel tasks than homogeneous groups – groups composed of members with similar backgrounds, etc.
Idea champion	A person who is committed, often personally, to the implementation of particular solution.
Ignoring commonalties	The failure to identify common features in apparently disparate things. A feature of the commitment block.
Illumination stage	The Eureka Moment or the third stage in the innovation cycle, when an insight is recognised and effectively articulated.
Incubation stage	An early stage in the thinking process or innovation cycle, sometimes known as 'sleeping on it', when unconscious mental activity combines and builds to produce a potential solution.
Lateral thinking	A term coined by deBono for a thinking process that involves 'moving sideways' and not continuing in a sequential process. (cf. Vertical thinking). DeBono likens it to using the reverse gear on a car – not for use all the time but essential when you need to get out of tight corners.
Left hemisphere thinking	A concept derived from a probable simplification of the way the human brain functions. It is implied that logical, analytical, linear or sequential thought comes from activity in the left hemisphere of the brain.
Morphological forced connections	A technique which seeks to combine logical and creative thought processes. The process constructs a matrix where properties or attributes form one dimension, and areas of use the other. Each 'box' of the matrix is then tested for an 'idea' or 'application'. Thus, in looking for new uses of glass, the properties could be listed as transparency, light bending, brittleness and hardness, and the areas of use as home, industry, whilst the other 'box' could well be surface polishing.

Neuro Linguistic Programming (NLP)	A major contribution to understanding human communications made by Richard Bandler and John Grinder. One part is concerned with 'thinking languages'.
Perceptual stereotyping	Problem definition using unquestioned preconceptions.
Personal analogies	A synectic problem-solving technique in which individuals ask: 'If I was involved with the situation, how would I feel, what help would I need?'
Potential problem analysis	A technique developed by Kepner and Tregoe whereby 'brainstorming' is used to collect the problems that COULD occur in the implementation of a potential solution.
Preparation stage	The first stage in the thinking process or innovation cycle when data is being collected, the problem is being defined and the 'obvious' alternatives are being collected and evaluated.
Rational problem-solving	A system of problem-solving based on four steps: 1. Defining the problem – constraints and standards to be achieved. 2. Generating alternatives. 3. Evaluating the alternatives against the constraints and standards. Selecting a tentative solution. 4. Implementation including contingency planning.
Reversing the definition	A tool for expanding problem definition by reversing the current way of thinking about a problem, e.g., 'The problem is to get the bones out of the fish. How about re-defining the problem as getting the fish flesh off the bones?'
Right hemisphere	A concept derived from a probable simplification of the way the human brain functions. It is implied that holistic, intuitive, creative, qualitative thinking comes from activity in the right hemisphere of the brain.
Subdivision	Breaking problems into small parts.
Symbolic analogies	Symbols or images that are imposed on the problem; recommended as part of synectics.
Synectics	A major contribution to creative problem-solving originally proposed by Gordon and later developed by Prince. The technique makes great play on the use of analogy. A complete system encompassing a range of styles.
Thinking languages	The various ways in which a problem may be handled, probably reflecting the thinking process that makes an individual more confident. Words are the most obvious language but beyond words individuals think in images, pictures, sounds and feelings. By moving between the languages, problems can be solved more easily.
Thinking strategy	The method followed by individuals for interpreting or judging data. In this text we see it as a systematic route developed as a skill.

Verification stage   The final stage in creative thought whereby standards are applied to potential solutions.

Vertical thinking   A term probably coined by deBono implying a sequential thinking strategy which begins by defining a problem in a single way and continuing logically from that start point.

References

Allen, J. L. *Conceptual blockbusting*. San Francisco: W. H. Freeman, 1974.

Amabile, Teresa M. A model of creativity and innovation in organizations. In Cummings, Larry L. & Staw, Barry M. (Eds.), *Research in organizational behavior*, 1988, 10, 123-167.

Barron, F. X. *Creativity and psychological health*. New York: Van Nostrand, 1963.

Basadur, M. S. *Training in creative problem solving: Effects of deferred judgment and problem finding and solving in an industrial research organization*. Unpublished doctoral dissertation, University of Cincinnati, 1979.

Beveridge, W. *The art of scientific investigation*. New York: Random House, 1960.

Bower, M. Nurturing innovation in an organization. In G. A. Steiner (Ed.), *The creative organization*. Chicago: University of Chicago Press, 1965.

Broadwell, M. M. *The new supervisor*. Reading, Mass.: Addison-Wesley, 1972.

Bruner, J. S. *On knowing: Essays for the left hand*. Cambridge: Harvard University Press, 1966.

Buzan, T. *Use your head*. BBC Publications, 1974.

Campbell, N. *What is science?* New York: Dover, 1952.

Cialdini, Robert B. *Influence: Science and practice*. Glenview, Ill.: Scott Foresman, 1988.

Crovitz, H. F. *Galton's walk*. New York: Harper & Row, 1970.

Dauw, D. C. *Creativity and innovation in organisations*. Dubuque, Iowa; Kendall Hunt, 1976.

De Bono, E. *New think*. New York: Basic Books, 1968.

DeBono, E. *Lateral Thinking for Management*. McGraw Hill: New York and London, 1971.

Dellas, M. & Gaier, E. L. Identification of creativity: The individual. *Psychological Bulletin*, 1970, 73, 55-73.

Drucker, P. F. *Management*. Oxford: Butterworth Heinemann, 1974.

Einstein, A. *Fundamental ideas and methods of relativity theory, presented in their development*. (c. 1919, G. Holton.) Unpublished manuscript.

Elbing, A. *Behavioral decisions in organizations*. Glenview, Ill.: Scott Foresman, 1978.

Ettlie, John E. & O'Keefe, Robert D. Innovative attitudes, values, and intentions in organizations. *Journal of Management Studies*, 1982, 19, 163–182.

Feldman, D. *Why do clocks run clockwise?* New York: National Syndications, 1988.

Festinger, Leon. *A theory of cognitive dissonance*. Stanford: Stanford University Press, 1957.

Filley, A. C., House, R. J. & Kerr, S. *Managerial process and organizational behavior*. Glenview, Ill.: Scott Foresman, 1976.

Finneston, Montague. *Engineering our future*. London: HMSO, 1980.

Galbraith, Jay R. Designing the innovating organization. *Organizational Dynamics*, Winter 1982, 5–25.

Gardner, J. W. *Self-renewal*. New York: Harper & Row, 1965.

Geshka, H. Introduction and use of idea generation techniques in industry. *Creativity Network*, 1978, Vol 3, No 2, 3–6.

Gordon, W. J. J. *Synectics: The development of creative capacity*. New York: Collier, 1961.

Guilford, J. P. Creativity: Its measurement and development. In S. J. Parnes & H. F. Harding (Eds.), *A sourcebook for creative thinking*. New York: Scribner, 1962.

Haefele, J. W. *Creativity and innovation*. New York: Reinhold, 1962.

Handy, Charles. *The Empty Raincoat*. London: Hutchinson, 1994.

Heider, Fritz. Attitudes and cognitive organization. *Journal of Psychology*, 1946, 21, 107–112.

Hermann, N. The creative brain. *Training and Development Journal*, 1981.

Huber, G. P. *Managerial decision making*. Glenview, Ill.: Scott Foresman, 1980.

Hudson, Liam. *Contrary imaginations*. Harmondsworth: Penguin, 1966.

Interaction Associates. *Tools for change*. San Francisco: Interaction Associates, 1971.

Janis, Irvin L. *Groupthink*. New York: Free Press, 1971.

Kanter, Rosabeth M. *The change masters*. London: Routledge, 1983.

Kepner, C. H. and Tregoe, B. B. *The rational manager*. McGraw-Hill, 1965.

Koestler, A. *The act of creation*. New York: Dell, 1967.

Maier, N. R. F. Assets and liabilities of group problem solving: The need for an integrative function. *Psychological Review*, 1967, 74, 239–249.

Maier, N. R. F. *Problem solving and creativity in individuals and groups*. Belmont, Calif.: Brooks/Cole, 1970.

March, J. G. & Simon, H. A. *Organizations*. New York: Wiley, 1958.

Markoff, John. For scientists using supercomputers, visual imagery speeds discoveries. New York Times News Service, *Ann Arbor News*, 2 Nov., 1988.

Martindale, C. What makes creative people different. *Psychology Today*, 1975, 9, 44-50.

McKim, R. H. *Experiences in visual thinking*. Monterey, Calif.: Brooks/Cole, 1972.

McMillan, Ian. *Progress in research on corporate venturing*. Working paper, Center for Entrepreneurial Studies, New York University, 1985.

Medawar, P. B. *The art of the soluble*. London: Methuen, 1967.

Nayak, P. R. & Ketteringham, John M. *Breakthroughs!* New York: Rawson Associates, 1986.

Nemeth, C. J. Differential contributions of majority and minority influence. *Psychological Review*, 1986, 93, 23-32.

Newcomb, Theodore. An approach to the study of communicative acts. *Psychological Review*, 1954, 60, 393-404.

Oakland, John S. *Total quality management*. Oxford: Butterworth Heinemann, 1994.

Osborn, A. *Applied imagination*. New York: Scribner, 1953.

Parnes, S. J. Can creativity be increased? In S. J. Parnes & H. F. Harding (Eds.), *A sourcebook for creative thinking*. New York: Scribner, 1962.

Raudsepp, G. P. & Hough, Jr. *Creative Growth Games*. New York: Putman, 1977.

Raudsepp, Eugene. *How Creative Are You?* New York: Putnam, 1981.

Rickards, Tudor. *Problem solving through creative analysis*. London: Gower, 1974.

Rickards, Tudor. *Creativity and problem solving at work*. London: Gower, 1988.

Rothenberg, A. Creative contradictions. *Psychology Today*, 1979, 13, 55-62.

Schumacher, E. F. *A guide for the perplexed*. New York: Harper & Row, 1977.

Scott, Otto J. *The creative ordeal: The story of Raytheon*. New York: Atheneum, 1974.

Steiner, G. *The creative organization*. Chicago: University of Chicago Press, 1978.

Tannenbaum, R. & Schmidt, W. H. How to choose a leadership pattern. *Harvard Business Review*, 1958, 3, 95-101.

Taylor, C. W. & Barron, F. X. *Scientific creativity: Its recognition and development*. New York: Wiley, 1963.

Thamia, S. A. & Woods, M. F. A small group approach to creativity and innovation. *R&D Management*, 14, 1, 1984.

Thompson, J. D. & Tuden, A. Strategies, structures, and processes or organizational decision. In J. D. Thompson & A. Tuden (Eds.),

Comparative studies in administration. Pittsburgh: University of Pittsburgh Press, 1959.

Tichy, Noel. *Strategic human resource management*. New York: Wiley, 1983.

Torrance, E. P. Scientific views of creativity and factors affecting its growth. *Daedalus*, 1965, 94, 663–682.

Twiss, Brian. *Managing technological innovation*. London: Longman, 1980.

von Oech, Roger. *A kick in the seat of the pants*. New York: Harper & Row, 1986.

Vroom, V. H. & Yetton, P. W. *Leadership and decision making*. Pittsburgh: University of Pittsburgh Press, 1973.

Vygotsky, L. *Thought and language.* Cambridge, Mass.: MIT Press, 1962.

Weick, K. E. *The social psychology of organizing*. Reading, Mass.: Addison-Wesley, 1979.

Index

Allen, J. L., 23, 35, 52
Amabile, M., 71
Amana Refrigeration Company, 33
analogy, 55
assumptions
    boundaries, 42
    dominant ideas, 42
    polarising factors, 42
    tethering factors, 42

Barron, F. X., 24
Basadur, M. S., 51, 52
Bell, Alexander Graham, 30
Beveridge, W., 38
bias against thinking, 48
Bibliotheque Nationale, 87
Birds Eye, 54
Bohr, Niels, 56
Bower, M., 25
brainstorming, 62
    role of facilitator, 63
Bruner, J. S., 49
Buzan, T
    mind mapping, 64

Campbell, N., 54
case studies
    Bleak Future of Knowledge, 86
    Sony Walkman, 81
Cavity Magnetron, 26
CEDAC, 64
Cialdini, R. B., 29
Cockcroft, Sir John, 26, 36
conceptual blockbusting, 51
conceptual blocks, 22, 23, 28
    blockbusting, 51
    commitment, 28, 35
    complacency, 29, 47
    compression, 29, 40, 44
    consistency, 28, 29
    review of, 51

stereotyping – defending the status
    quo, 35
creative problem-solving
    assumption cf., 43
    behavioural guidelines, 78
    brainstorming, 62
    deferring judgement, 62
    elaboration of the definition, 57
    fishbone techniques, 64
    generating more alternatives, 62
    hints for application, 67
    ignoring commonalities, 38
    impediments to, 22
    improved problem definition, 53
    making the strange familiar, 54
    model for, 70
    moving outside the square, 41
    power of training, 25
    relational algorithm, 66
    relation to children, 23
    seeing the wood for the trees, 43
    stages of creative thought, 52
    subdivision, 64
    use of analogy and metaphor, 55
Crovitz, H. F., 66

Data General, 72
Dauw, D. C., 52
De Bono, 25, 29, 42, 43, 59
    assumption analysis, 25
Dellas, M. & Gaier, E. L., 38, 66
Dolby sound, 77
Drucker, P. F., 18

Eagle project, 72
effective implementation
    attributes of quality, 18
Einstein, A., 61
Elbing, A., 20
evaluation and selection
    attributes of quality, 16

exercises
  ambidextrous principle, 50
  brainstorm, 63
  embedded patterns, 45
  five figure problem, 58
  fractionation problem, 66
  ignoring commonalities, 38
  Roman IX, 34
  seven matches, 34
  the block problem, 39
  the nine dot problem, 40
  the Shakespeare volumes, 37
  the story of the pebbles, 59

Festinger, L., 29
Filley, A. C., House, R. J. & Kerr, S., 20
Finneston Report, 77
Fleming, Sir Alexander, 38
Foerstner, George, 33, 44
Ford Motor Company EQUIP
  programme, 43
Fry, Art, 33, 39

Galbraith, J. K., 71
Getting, Ivan, 32
Gordon, 54
Guilford, J. P., 51, 52

Haefele, J. W., 52
Handy, Charles, 25
Harvey, William, 56
Heider, F., 29
Hermann, N., 49
Huber, G. P., 20

idea champion, 75
innovativeness
  monitor and prod, 73
  principles for, 70
  pull people apart, put them together,
    71
  reward multiple roles, 75
Interaction Associates, 53
IQ test, 52
Ishikawa, 64

Janis, I. L., 72
Jansky, Karl, 30
Janusian thinking, 61

Johnson Controls, 73

Kanter, R. M., 71
Kekule, Fredrich, 38
Kentucky Fried Chicken, 30
Kepner, C. H. & Tregoe, B. B., 20
Ketteringham, J. M., 83
Koestler, A., 32, 38

lateral thinking, 29
left-hemisphere thinking, 49
libraries
  bleak future, 86
Library of Congress, 86

3M, 27, 44, 73
Maier, N. R. F., 20, 29, 63
March, J. G. & Simon, H. A., 16, 35, 62,
  65
Markoff, J., 34
Martindale, C., 49
McKim, R. H., 39, 52
McMillan, 71
Medawar, P. B., 54
microwave oven, 27, 36
Milky Way galaxy, 30
mind mapping, 64
Miskolc, 48
Mitsuro, I., 81
model of rational and creative
  problem-solving, 70

Nayak, P. R. & Ketteringham, J. M., 27,
  33, 34, 37, 39, 44
Nemeth, C. J., 72
Newcomb, T., 29

Oakland, J., 47, 64
Osborn, A., 62

Parnes, S. J.
  power of training, 25
Pauling, L., 46
Pepys, Samuel, 48
Post-It Notes, 28, 31, 33, 75
Potters–Ballontini, 25
Puxxles, 47

radar, 26, 36

radio astronomy, 30
Randall, J. & Boot, H., 26
rational problem-solving
    implementation, 18
    limitations, 20
Raytheon, 26
Rickards, T
    Puxxles, 47
right-hemisphere thinking, 49
Rothenberg, D. L., 60, 61
Rutherford, Lord, 56

Sanders, Colonel, 30
Schumacher, E. F., 54
Scott, O. J., 32
Silver, Spence, 27, 31, 33, 37, 73
snag lists, 48
Sony Corporation, 81
Sony Pressman, 81
Spencer, Percy, 26, 31, 32, 36, 73
stages in creative thought, 52
Steiner, G., 38, 51
Sumitomo Electric, 64
Synectics, 54

use of analogy, 55

Tezuka, Takichi, 81
Tannenbaum, R. & Schmidt, W. H., 18
Taylor, C. W. & Barron, F. X., 24
Thamia, S. & Woods, M., 19, 67
The Economist, 87
thinking language, 31
Thompson, J. D. & Tuden, A., 20
Tichy, N., 71
Torrance, E. P., 24
Total Quality Systems, 64

Unilever, 31

vertical thinking, 29
von Oech, Roger, 56
Vroom, V. H. & Yetton, P. W., 18
Vygotsky, L., 32

Weick, Karl, 53

Yorkshire pudding, 36